Praise for "With Courage Shall We Fight"

Holocaust survivors Fruma Gulkowich Berger and Murray "Motke" Berger, two resistance fighters, husband and wife, write in poetry and prose of their experiences. Their sons offer a loving introduction and a prologue, but the heart of their story is a memoir of pain and anguish, defiance, determinaton and resistance, which gives ample testimony not only to courage and to bravery, but a unique type of courage born of despair and desperation. A powerful work.

Michael Berenbaum
Professor Jewish Studies
American Jewish University, Los Angeles, CA

A rare work that combines both compelling narrative and beautiful poetry and prose, this important book offers profound insight into a distant era about the intersection of two lives. The poem, "I Am the Last," left me with shivers, the phrase "I am the last to remember where my house was, the last to remember those I loved so well," deeply moved me. Although I've looked at the famous Bielski photograph of Fruma Gulkowich Berger so many times, I never realized this person with a machine gun in her lap was in fact a woman, whose words would one day move and inspire me. The collection of written work by the editors at the end makes it even more of a treasure.

Mitch Braff, Executive Director
Jewish Partisan Educational Foundation
San Francisco, CA

With Courage Shall We Fight presents a most fascinating and compelling account of Murray and Fruma Berger's incredible experience during the Holocaust as part of the Bielski partisans resistance group. This wonderful memoir of poetry combined with a well written narrative history serves as an excellent resource for educators to use as a primary document when teaching the Holocaust.

Resistance in the Holocaust took many forms but this collection of such heartfelt and sincere poetry is a form of spiritual resistance that is one of a kind. Truly a touching memoir and a must read for anyone who is a serious student of the Holocaust and Resistance.

Dr. Miriam Klein Kassenoff, Director
University of Miami Holocaust Teacher Institute and
Education Co-Chair of The Holocaust Memorial: Miami Beach, Florida

WITH COURAGE
Shall We Fight

The Memoirs and Poetry of Holocaust Resistance Fighters

FRANCES "FRUMA" GULKOWICH BERGER
MURRAY "MOTKE" BERGER

Edited by
Ralph S. Berger & Albert S. Berger

C⊙MTEQ PUBLISHING
MARGATE, NEW JERSEY

Royalties from the sales of this book will benefit the Museum of Jewish Heritage in New York City.

Published by:
    ComteQ Publishing
    A division of ComteQ Communications, LLC
    101 N. Washington Ave. • Suite 1B
    Margate, New Jersey 08402
    609-487-9000 • Fax 609-487-9099
    Email: publisher@ComteQpublishing.com
    Website: www.ComteQpublishing.com

ISBN 978-1-935232-20-9
Library of Congress Control Number: 2010929504

Book and cover design by Rob Huberman

Cover photo: Partisans after the war - Kibbutz Tulda, Romania, 1945. Murray Berger, center first row, Fruma Berger, third row center.

Printed in the United States of America

Acknowledgments

Dedicated to Sam Pogorelsky, for whom the compilation of this book was a labor of love.

Special thanks go to Esther Crystal for editing the manuscript, Dr. Michael Berenbaum and Bonnie Gurewitsch for their review and constructive comments, Prof. Larry Gillig, the late Dr. Percy Matenko, Zelik Bedell, Sam Pogorelsky, Sheryl Kohl and Pearl Rochelson for translating the Yiddish poems, Shoshana Rosenblum for doing the Yiddish typing, Patricia Bartels for proofreading, and Phil and Dorota Feinzeig for their help in finding the Novogrudek area map.

Contents

Foreward 9

The Bielski Brigade: A Brief History 11

Map 14

The Testimony of Fruma Gulkowich Berger -
In Her Own Words 15

The Testimony of Murray Berger –
In His Own Words 32

The Poetry of Fruma Gulkowich Berger 48

"Tears and Poems of a Jewish Woman" 95

"A Jew from the Forests" 102

Afterword: In the Words of their Children -
Ralph S. Berger and Albert S. Berger 106

The Story of Two Lives - A Photo Album 118

Endnotes 143

Sources 144

Glossary 145

Foreward

*Tell your children of it and let your children
tell their children, and their children another
generation....*Joel 1:3

With *courage shall we fight*, a line from one of our mother's poems, "Jewish Partisans," is a fitting title for the memoir of Murray "Motke" and Frances "Fruma" Gulkowich Berger's incredible story of survival. Miraculously, first individually and then together as fighters in the Bielski Brigade, they escaped from the Nazis and certain death and literally fought back, saving not only their own lives but those of others as well.

Those fortunate enough to have known our parents understood that their history was more than a story of survival during the Holocaust, of enduring the hardships of displaced persons, and of establishing themselves in a new country where they had arrived nearly broke and barely speaking the language. Theirs was a love story.

Our parents did not just have a marriage. They had a romance that lasted for over fifty years. We recently listened to a radio interview that our parents gave in 1986. We pictured Dad smiling slyly as he told the interviewer, Norman Lester, how he "found" his wife "in the woods." Mom spoke of how love "can blossom" under even the most adverse circumstances. The love, respect and admiration they had for each other helped to sustain them and to overcome numerous hardships for the rest of their lives. We find it difficult to understand how two individuals who experienced such loss and witnessed the horrors of the Holocaust could still be such warm, giving people.

There wasn't a day in our lives when we did not feel our parents' love. And it wasn't reserved just for us. Close friends and extended family members were also included. Visitors to our parents' house always felt at home.

It is our hope that this memoir will teach future generations about courage in the face of adversity and that the experiences of our parents—and those of other Holocaust martyrs and survivors—must never be forgotten.

Ralph S. Berger and Albert S. Berger

The Bielski Brigade: A Brief History

The Holocaust impacted the lives of all European Jews. But Polish Jews, in particular, suffered more than most since they were in an especially vulnerable region. Situated between Russia and Germany, Poland had been an area of contention between the two countries for many years.

At the end of WWI, Russia had received more than half of Poland as compensation for its losses. During the early portion of WWII, Russia and Germany were allies. This situation changed radically in the summer of 1941 when Germany attacked and badly defeated Russia, resulting in Germany regaining the half of Poland that had been in Russian hands.

After having suffered years of Russian anti-Semitism, the Polish Jews who lived in this territory now became prime targets of the Nazi anti-Jewish measures and the Final Solution.[i] Jewish areas were declared ghettos and the Jews in them were effectively trapped. Faced with the choice of certain annihilation by the Nazis if they stayed in the ghetto, some Jews took their chances and escaped into the forests to join the partisans.

The forests around Russian-Poland (Belorussia) had been the site of a Russian partisan movement ever since Russia's rout by Germany. Thousands of Russian soldiers—former POWs, deserters and Belorussian men—escaped to the forests.[ii] This development was useful to the Soviet government, which saw it as an opportunity to mobilize their ex-soldiers in the forest to fight the Germans from within. Specially trained units were sent by the Soviet Central Committee of the Communist Party to initiate and support guerilla activities against German troops in the area.

Jewish ghetto runaways thought that the Russian partisans would give them protection, but this was not usually the case. While some Jews who fled into the forests were absorbed into the Russian partisan units, often, even armed Jewish men weren't permitted to join the Russian *otriads* (units).[iii] There were a number of reasons for this—deeply entrenched Russian anti-Semitism and the intrinsically different aims of the two groups. For the Russian partisans, the ultimate purpose of conducting guerilla activities was to defeat the Germans. For the Jewish partisans, the ultimate purpose was twofold—to survive and to help other Jews survive. [iv]

Some Jews who fled to the Naliboki forest of Western Belorussia created their own Jewish partisan unit, known as the Bielski detachment. The Bielski detachment was founded by the Bielski brothers—Tuvia, Alexander Zisel "Zus" and Asael—who had managed to flee to the forest after their parents and other family members were killed in the ghetto massacres in December of 1941. Along with 14 other men who had also escaped from the Novogrudek ghetto (including Murray Berger and Ben-Zion Gulkowich) they formed the nucleus of this new partisan combat group, with Tuvia Bielski as its commander.

While the Bielski detachment was originally conceived as a separate Jewish partisan unit and functioned as such until the last quarter of 1942, by 1943 the Bielski Brigade was participating in joint military ventures with the Russian partisans. By then, the Bielski Brigade had gained legitimacy within the Russian partisan movement and additionally, the Soviet partisan movement had adopted a more liberal recruitment policy thereby allowing more Jewish participation.[v]

The Bielski *otriad* was nominally under the command of General Platon (Vasily Yehimovich Chernyshev) but was never fully absorbed into the Soviet partisan movement because the Bielski Brigade wanted to retain its integrity. Eventually, the Soviet partisan leaders split the group into two units, one named Ordzhonikidze in which Zus was head of reconnaissance, and one named Kalinin led by Tuvia. Bielski fighters from both units killed a total of 381 enemy fighters, sometimes during joint actions with Soviet groups. The main purpose of the Bielski Brigade, however, was to give protection to Jewish fugitives. Hundreds of men, women, and children eventually found their way to the Bielski camp.

The group followed the established pattern of other partisan units. The Bielski partisans lived in *ziemlankas* (underground dugouts). After dark, they would venture into the village to get food from the local peasants. They could not stay in one area for any great length of time as they needed to collect food from the different farms in the area and also needed to avoid being reported to the Germans.

Bielski partisans made forays into the Novogrudek ghetto to rescue others, to check on relatives, and to gather weapons. There were differing opinions among the partisans over recruitment.[vi] Tuvia consistently wanted to expand the group. He stated that he "would rather save one old Jewish woman than kill ten German soldiers." Other Jewish partisans saw their purpose as exacting revenge from the Germans by killing as many as possible. In spite of the enormous dangers, they managed to do both. The Bielski detachment grew into a forest community of more than 1200 and distinguished itself as the most massive rescue operation of Jews by Jews.

The Bielski partisan group existed until the summer of 1944, when the Soviet counteroffensive began in Belorussia and the area was liberated.[vii]

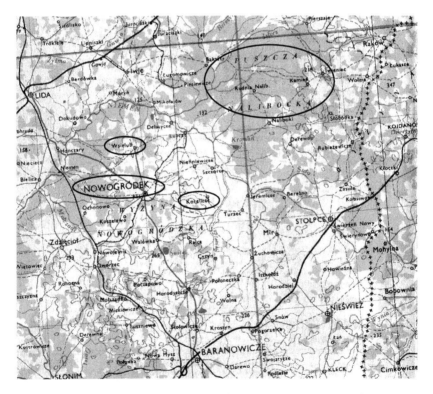

A map of the area where Murray and Fruma Berger lived and fought.

The Testimony of Fruma Gulkowich Berger — In Her Own Words

Before the War

I was born Fruma Gulkowich in Lublin, Poland in 1918. When I was very small, my parents moved the family to the town of Korelitz, which was located in the Polish county of Novogrudek in the Eastern part of Poland (Belorussia). The town had about 1500 Jews. The older generation maintained a pious Jewish life; the younger generation was more active in cultural groups and the Zionist movement.

My father was in business—different ones at different times—and my mother helped him out. We had a house and a big garden where we grew vegetables of all kinds. We had our own cow and a horse for transportation.

We were four sisters and one brother. We spoke Yiddish in the house, Russian in the street and Polish in school. My father was very religious and we kept all the traditions. I had

15

Christian friends in school but most of my friends were Jewish.

There was anti-Semitism when I was growing up. Boys threw stones at us and beat us up. Then in the 1930s, the anti-Semitism got worse. Gentiles from the area would break windows and call us all kinds of names. Closer to 1939, they stopped buying from Jewish stores altogether.

My sisters and I were active in the Zionist movement. I belonged to the *Halutz* and *Shomer Hatza'ir* youth groups. We wanted to emigrate from Poland. All the youth wanted to go to Palestine. One of my sisters was already making *"hachshara"* — preparation for going to Palestine. At that time, it was impossible to get a certificate to go to Palestine; because of the British Mandate they were restricting immigration. My sister waited six to eight months for a certificate to go. She wanted to join a kibbutz. But by then it was too late.

We felt that if we couldn't emigrate to Palestine, we would try to go to South Africa because my mother had three sisters there. I had a visa to go there but then the war broke out and the door was closed. I remained with my family in Korelitz.

Then came very bad times. When the Russians and the Germans started fighting in 1939, the Russians entered Korelitz and occupied it. They began operating Soviet-style in our town. They nationalized the larger buildings, including my parents' house that was not even big enough for our family, yet they installed another family of seven to live together with us. They closed down all the stores and set up one large one. You couldn't have a private business. There was a shortage of commodities and lines formed for supplies.

All adults had to go to work. We were put to work in co-operatives. I was lucky to get a job in an office. Somehow we got used to this kind of life, hoping that the war would end soon and things would get better. But things got a lot worse.

The ghetto and the massacres

On June 22, 1941, the Nazis invaded Korelitz. I will never forget that day. The bombing started and we were looking for a place to hide. It didn't last too long, but soon our town was besieged by the Nazis and they started their war against the Jews.

The town became chaotic. From the surrounding villages, peasants came with sacks and empty wagons and started looting Jewish houses. We couldn't stay in our house. We had to give the Nazis and their collaborators our valuables. We were not treated as human beings anymore; all our possessions were taken away from us. We were locked in a few houses under police guard and that was the first ghetto. We had to wear a yellow patch on our clothing. All able men and women were ordered to report to work and we were "escorted" by police back and forth from the ghetto. We had to do all the hard and dirty work—street cleaning, working in factories, other hard work.

The Nazis established a government in town and gave their orders through the *Judenrat*. We wanted to escape to Russia but we didn't know what was happening there. The Nazis were so quick and the Russian cities were already burning.

Within a few weeks, the SS came to our town. They ordered us to gather in the marketplace where the Nazis made a selection. They called the names from a list that was prepared for them by our Polish "good" neighbors. They took 105 of the youngest, strongest, smartest men, and took them to the synagogue and locked them up overnight. The next day, a bus came and took them. They were supposed to be taken to the next city to work but within a few days we found out from our non-Jewish neighbors that they were all murdered. The Nazis and their helpers came around to their families to ask for money for food for them but we knew that they weren't alive any more.

One day, in the first ghetto in Korelitz while we were at work, the local police, who were Nazi collaborators headed by Briczkowsky, came into the house looking for gold. They believed all Jews were hiding gold. My mother was home and she had a compress on her face because she had a bad toothache. They said she was pretending to have a toothache so she wouldn't have to go to work and they beat her up very badly. When we came home from work we found her full of blood, beaten around the head, with her face severely bruised. We wanted to take her to the hospital in Novogrudek and we set out but we had to turn back after people told us about the slaughter that was going on there. My mother died within a few weeks of her wounds. She was 58 years old.

In May 1942, the ghetto in Korelitz was merged with the ghetto in Novogrudek. We all had to go to the marketplace with whatever few belongings we had and stand in rows of four in the Korelitz market square. Those who would not come out were shot on the spot. We were encircled by armed police. I was in the first row, together with my three sisters, Grunia, Feigele and Brina, and my father—whose feet were badly swollen on account of malnutrition. My brother Ben-Zion and his wife Judy "Yehudis" were standing behind us. My two little nieces, Mirele and Hayale, my married sister's child and my brother's child, were also there.

Surrounded by SS men and Nazi police, we were forced to march. Children who were too young to walk had to be carried. Late in the day, almost by nightfall, we came to the city of Novogrudek and the slave labor ghetto, our second ghetto.

Novogrudek was a concentration ghetto—Jews from other towns in the vicinity of Novogrudek were also driven into this ghetto at this time. In pain, hungry, and thirsty, we were driven like dogs into stalls in the Peresica Ghetto of Novogrudek. The Jews of Novogrudek were already there, as well as Jews from the surrounding towns of Lubtsh, Ivenitse, Nalibok, Wseilub, Delatycz, Naisztot and others.

Our living quarters were in the barns previously used as stables for horses and cattle. Under horrible, unsanitary conditions and much overcrowding, we were barely able to stay alive. The worst of all was the hunger, and the very hard work we were forced to perform. The young and able-bodied were taken to work camps in the morning and brought back by nightfall under Nazi police escort.

Our sufferings were greater than those endured by the Jews of Novogrudek because we did not know anyone. A Jewish policeman from the ghetto had flogged me because I wanted to go to work with a group from Novogrudek. I wanted to go with them because perhaps someone would have pity on me and throw me a piece of bread. On another occasion, a policeman caught me entering the ghetto with a piece of bread hidden under my dress. I was arrested and put in jail.

Abuses and murders were going on every day in the ghetto. We wanted to escape and a few people did, but we were always under guard and we didn't know where to escape to. My brother, Ben-Zion, tried to organize a group to go look for partisans to join, but the *Judenrat* was against it because the Nazis had announced that if a single Jew was not accounted for, a whole group would be slaughtered. When he first tried to escape to the forest with a group of others, they took away his boots to prevent him from leaving the ghetto.

In the summer of 1942, one could feel in the air that something was being prepared. On August 6, 1942, my sisters and I were walking towards the gate to go to work. At that time, we were working in the center of the city cleaning up the rubble of the buildings that were bombed when the Nazis first invaded. We had a feeling that any day the Nazis would surround the ghetto. My niece, a six-year-old girl, was asking me to take her with me. I agreed and was successful because the policeman at the gate turned a blind eye. It seemed that there was a little more ease at work.

Suddenly there was panic. People started to run in all directions. We started to run also. No one knew where to run. We heard that the ghetto was surrounded. My sister-in-law Judy and I ran together, not knowing where we were going. We ran to the military barracks, because many ran in that direction. The SS rounded up all the fleeing Jews, including me and Judy, and started to "select" by pointing with the finger; to the left meant death, to the right meant life. We had heard about this already. All of the women were sent to the left, some men to the right, and the rest of the men were shot in front of us. With their rifles pointed at us, they then marched us back to the Peresica ghetto under a police guard made up of Byelorussians, Ukrainians, Lithuanians and others.

It was getting dark and the ghetto was surrounded by Nazis. The ghetto was very quiet by that time, as if the Angel of Death had already spread its wings. I went into the barn where we had been staying. It was nearly empty. My sisters had already found a hiding place in an attic. My father was standing near the bunk in his *tallis* reciting *Tehilim*. He looked at me as if he were saying goodbye with his eyes. He did not say a word; I turned to stone. I will never forget how he looked at me.

When my sister-in-law Judy saw me standing there frozen, she hit me on the arm and said, "What are we waiting for? Let's go out of the barn before it is too late and find some hole to hide in." I couldn't look back. I never saw my father or my sisters again.

We walked through the ghetto passing by dead bodies. One of them I recognized as a girl from our town, Mirke Jelen. She had the courage to spit in the face of a Nazi. We passed the big outhouse in the center of the ghetto and without any hesitation, we decided that would be our hiding place.

We went in and lowered ourselves down into the large cesspool of human waste. The waste was up to my chest. There were already two women inside: Ester Menaker and Masza Rabinowicz. We each went into a separate corner, so that in case the SS men should look in there, if the breathing of one was heard, the others might not be discovered. The night passed without any disturbances with us shivering in fear of the expectation of the coming morning.

On Friday, August 7, 1942, early in the morning, I heard the noise of buses coming into the ghetto and then the Germans shouting, *"Schneller, schneller, verfluchte Juden! Raus, raus!"* ("Faster, faster, cursed Jews! Get out here, get out here!") Dogs were barking and little children were crying out, "Where are you, Mother?" These last cries still ring in my ears. The children were herded onto buses and then gassed in the buses, among them my two little nieces.

After the Nazis chased all the Jews out into the center of the ghetto, they were ordered to lie down and were beaten without mercy. The Jews were then placed on trucks and driven to Litovka, where a huge mass grave in the form of a large ditch had already been dug. The Jews were ordered off the trucks and marched to the ditch. They were ordered to take off their clothes and then to walk onto a board placed across the deep ditch. They were then machine-gunned, group after group. Some put up resistance and started to run, but Nazi shots reached them anyway. A wounded man managed to escape from the mass grave and later on told me what had happened.

Down in the outhouse, I heard the shooting of 4,000 innocent people, among them my father, my three sisters, and many close relatives—around 70 people. Of my whole town, only a few survived. In the ghetto, music was playing and a voice from a loudspeaker was broadcasting, "To murder the Jews is a noble thing to God for every good Christian."

Suddenly I heard Germans talking and dogs barking near the outhouse. I feared that our hiding place had been discovered. At that moment I lay down deeper in the dirt of the cesspool so that the waste would cover me up. The SS men shot into the cesspool. A bullet hit the woman next to me. She was wearing a white coat and she was a heavy woman and was having a hard time breathing. They probably heard her heavy breathing and they shot her. Another bullet went through my clothing and slightly grazed my right arm. The Germans withdrew, saying to each other that anyone still alive in the cesspool would die there anyway and were not worth any more bullets.

We remained in the waste for six days without food or water. Big worms were crawling all over me and biting my body. The burning of my skin was unbearable.

On the sixth day they brought back the surviving Jews from the military barracks. Among them was my brother, Ben-Zion. The ghetto was reduced in size and we found ourselves outside of what was now the ghetto. They were working on the ghetto walls to make the ghetto smaller and it so happened that a man assigned to build the wall of the smaller ghetto had come to the outhouse for his needs. I saw the yellow patch so I started to speak to him. At first he got scared. Then he bent down and he saw us. I told him who we were and that if he saw my brother, Ben-Zion—we didn't even know if he was in the ghetto—to tell him that there were three women still alive including Fruma and Judy and to tell him that we were in the outhouse.

The man got word to him and the next day my brother Ben-Zion took a big risk and came to rescue us. He bribed a guard and then jumped over the ghetto wall and dragged all three of us from the cesspool. If another guard had seen him, he would have been shot. I could hardly stand on my feet, and no one could stand close to us from the dirt and the smell. I had wounds all over me. It was then that we realized the magnitude of the destruction.

We decided that we had to escape. We got news in the ghetto, through a letter delivered by a Christian neighbor, that the Bielski brothers, who were already in the forests, had started to organize a partisan group. My future husband Murray (whom I had not met yet) left the ghetto in the first group of eight men. With the second group, my brother Ben-Zion left. A few weeks later, he sneaked back into the ghetto for his wife Judy and me and to rescue other Jews.

On a dark and windy night in late August of 1942 we made our move to leave the ghetto. With us there came along thirty more Jews. We had heard stories of what the Nazis were doing and knew of the dangers that lay before us. With the German guards watching the ghetto all the time we had to be extremely cautious.

When we were already on the other side of the wall, maybe half a mile, we heard shots in our direction. Somehow we were lucky and we made it. It would be nice to say that God helped us and that it was a miracle. But if God could see the little babies thrown into the fire or thrown down from tall buildings or smashed against a tree like toys, then I couldn't believe in such a God.

In the Forest

After walking the whole night we came to the forest where the Bielski group stayed. There were around sixty people in the group at that time.

The forest became our home for two years. Life in the woods was difficult. Our group, the Bielski Brigade, was under the command of Tuvia Bielski and was growing fast, reaching twelve hundred Jews by the end of the war.

As our group grew, food was a constant problem. The only way to get it was to go out at night to the distant villages and ask the farmers. Some were willing to give; from others it had to be taken by force.

Security was another big problem. We could not stay in the same place too long. In the summer it was easier, but in the winter it was really miserable. In the summer we slept in tents, but in the winter we had to build bunkers underground called *ziemlankas*. On the surface they had to be camouflaged to appear as if nothing was underneath. They were without windows, without toilets, without fresh air to breathe. These were our sleeping quarters.

We had in our group people of all ages, even some children who miraculously escaped the massacres. Everyone was welcome, not as in the non-Jewish groups. Our unit was exclusively a Jewish partisan division. The Jewish groups believed in accepting everyone who could escape.

The first objective was to get ammunition. Some people had already secured guns in the ghetto; others who had some money in gold coins bought rifles from the peasants. In 1943, airplanes from Moscow dropped ammunition down to us. But mostly we got weapons by ambushing the enemy.

Since we could not engage in an open fight with the Nazis, we were mostly involved in sabotage work with homemade mines: blowing up bridges, railroad tracks, trains and all kinds of installations, and cutting telephone wires. It was very dangerous work and unfortunately many of our young people lost their lives.

We had scouts—one of them was Ben-Zion. He was the bravest. They would roam the forest on horseback, scour the farms and the villages in the area for information about the enemy, and then lay the groundwork for an attack.

The Jewish partisans had to engage in fights many times with Russian or Polish partisans, for they would quickly kill a

Jewish fighter for a good pair of boots or for a rifle. Some peasants were working for the Germans as informers. With their help and the local police, the Germans would very often raid the farms where partisans stopped to rest. Many brave young fighters met with cruel deaths as a result. Eventually, the informers received their punishment.

Many times the Germans encircled the forest with tanks and armored vehicles filled with soldiers. The forests were bombed and attacks were launched on the partisans' base. This was an *oblava* (raid). We were surrounded on all sides; danger was enormous. With such a big group as ours, and only a small amount of ammunition, we had to go to hideouts deeper in the swamps. For many days we did not have anything to eat or clean water to drink.

I was the first of the girls to get a rifle, and I would stand guard together with the men fighters, and I would join them in other acts of vengeance against the murderers of our people. Most of the women's work was cooking, washing, caring for the fellow partisans, and taking care of the sick and the wounded. I participated in those chores also.

For the women in the forest, mostly young girls, life was twice as hard. Beside the abominable conditions, we were constantly among men in a society where morality did not exist anymore. So most of us became close with a young man, and stayed together, and most are still living together now. I met my husband Murray in the forest. We fought together and we are together until this day. We got married after the war.

In the summer of 1944, I was standing on guard outside the base and I could hear the noise of explosions and guns far off, and I could see Russian planes flying over the forest. The Red Army passed on the road close to our base.

My emotions at that moment were simply indescribable. The Germans were retreating. It would soon be the end of our struggle in the woods, but danger was still with us. A big group of German soldiers on horseback was moving toward our base, throwing grenades and shooting on all sides.

Fighting began. Everyone who had a rifle was on the battlefield. We lost ten of our best people. What an irony for it to happen on that day, July 9, 1944. However, the Nazis did not make their escape either.

After the war

On August 13, 1944, the Bielski partisan group emerged from the forest. Murray, his brother Ellie, Ben-Zion, Judy and I decided to go back to Poland. We returned to Novogrudek and stayed until the end of 1944. There, we cried over the mass graves because what else could we do.

Murray, Ellie, Ben-Zion, Judy and I then went to Lublin, Poland where we met representatives from the *Bricha*—the Jewish illegal underground that was helping people get to Palestine. We were hoping to be on *Aliyah Bet* and get to Palestine illegally. We were traveling without documents, so everything had to be done illegally. The *Bricha* arranged for us to leave Poland for Romania.

In Romania, along with other former partisans and survivors of the concentration camps, we lived in a DP camp we called "Kibbutz Tulda." The five of us stayed in Romania until May 8, 1945 and then went to Austria by truck. But we only stayed there one day and then left for Italy.

We wanted to be in Italy because it was near the sea. We hoped to get on an illegal boat to Palestine. We stayed in a few places—Santa Caesaria and then Rome. In Rome, I married my husband, Murray, in a big synagogue on the Tiber River.

While we were in the DP camp in Italy, Kibbutz Anzio, we met people from the U.S. who came to help us find our relatives. A reporter put a notice in the American newspapers

to help find Murray's brother, Harry, who had left Poland for
the U.S. before Murray was born. I tried to find my relatives in
South Africa, but I didn't remember their address. Harry sent us
an affidavit and Murray, Ellie and I came to the U.S. in 1947. Ben-
Zion and Judy came a year later, along with their son Albert who
was born in Rome.

We started a new life here. Our children—Albert and Ralph,
who carry our parents' names—were born in the U.S. Albert
was born in Brooklyn and Ralph was born in the Bronx.

I still can't understand why it happened. I had a religious
upbringing and I keep a kosher house. I light candles on Friday
night and my husband Murray goes to synagogue and we have
big Friday night dinners, but I can't believe anymore after
seeing what happened. Why did it have to happen to innocent
people who didn't do anything wrong?

Hadaske, the little orphan

Too many times have I heard in this country that the Jews of
Europe were passive and that they allowed themselves to be led
like sheep by the Nazis to the slaughterhouse. This is an insult
and an injustice to the memories of the martyrs. It is not true.

The Jewish communities were in no position to match the
armed strength of the Nazis or to check the vicious assaults by
their neighbors. The Jews in the towns and in the cities were
living as a minority among other nationalities. They were quiet,
pious Jews, hardworking people, carrying on their traditions
and trying to live in peace with their neighbors. But as soon as
the Nazis came everything changed.

There was a resistance; there were acts of heroism, and in
many cases, self-sacrifice. (Editor's Note: The story of Hadaske
the orphan related below is one such instance.)

It was in the ghetto Novogrudek in 1942 in the beginning of
summer. At that time, the Nazi conquerors undertook to make

our towns *Judenrein*. All the Jewish people from the towns around Novogrudek were driven into the concentration ghetto there for the final solution.

While I was there I met a very good friend of our family from Yeremitz, not far from our town Korelitz, Shiffra Harkavi, and her two little girls. The older one, Ruthie, was about five years old, the younger one Hadaske, was a baby, not yet a year old in a carriage.

At first when we met we were crying, looking at each other, and at the sub-human conditions surrounding us. Then the questions began: "Who is still alive?" I heard from her the very painful news that all the Jews from Yeremitz had already been massacred, many of our relatives among them.

Shiffra and some members of the Harkavi family had moved to Novogrudek before the German invasion. The Harkavis were a very wealthy and most respectable family. The parents, Avrom-Eli and Sheina, had five sons and one daughter. The third son, Tana, was married to Shiffra.

When war broke out between Germany and the Soviet Union in June 1941, Tana was mobilized into the Red Army, so Shiffra and their two little children were now living in the Novogrudek ghetto with Tana's sister Sara and her young son as well as one of the younger Harkavi brothers, Michel. They were all that were left from the big family Harkavi.

I would meet Shiffra almost every day after work. She would wait for me by the gate of the ghetto. Then one day she said to me, "I have to tell you a secret. I want you to know that we are going away in hiding to a Gentile family, Bobrowski. Somehow I have a premonition that you will survive. If the worst should happen to my family, maybe someone will survive, maybe a child. Please, watch out for the child. I trust you."

That was the last time I saw her. Very soon after, the worst came to the ghetto. On August 7, 1942 there was the second massacre and 4,000 Jews were slaughtered. When the murderers finished with their task, one of the townspeople told them that in the nearest village there were some Jews in hiding.

The Nazis went there and they uncovered the shelter where the Harkavi family was hiding. The Bobrowski house with all the people inside was burnt down. But the murderers overlooked two little girls who were playing someplace outside. Later on, the girls were taken to a Christian orphanage in Novogrudek.

I knew from Shiffra that the Bobrowskis had one little girl of their own. I assumed that the other little girl must be Hadaske, the younger one of Shiffra's girls. Because she could not talk yet when they went into hiding, Hadaske could play safely with the other children outside and not be identified as Jewish. My brother and I decided to keep it a secret for the time being.

After years of suffering and struggle for survival we lived to see the defeat of Hitler's empire. We were liberated from the forests in the middle of the summer of 1944 by the Red Army. When we came to Novogrudek, the first thing I did was to go to the orphanage to find Hadaske. I went there with Murray, who would later become my husband.

I was really lucky that day. The director of the orphanage was a woman, a teacher from Yeremitz, who remembered my family and me well and also my relatives from Yeremitz. But most importantly, she knew the Harkavi family.

I told her everything about Hadaske and that I would like to see her. Her answer was that she believed my story, but she would have to make sure. If I could recognize the little girl then she would know that what I told her was correct.

She called all the little girls into the room, put them in a line and I had to decide which one was Hadaske. They were all dressed alike and almost all looked the same with blonde hair.

I looked from one face to the other. Most of them were laughing. But one had tears in her eyes and did not want to raise her head. Finally she looked at me and at that moment, in my mind, I heard Shiffra talking to me and saw her face.

I did not hesitate any longer and pointed out that little girl. I was right. She was at that time approximately three-and-a-half years old. The director just said, "The children always call her 'Jewess (Zydowka)'." She was registered there under the name of Halinka Bobrowski so I asked the woman in charge to change her name to her real one, and she did. I would then go every day to the orphanage and bring Hadaske some clothing, some food, whatever I could spare.

The war was still going on. We were free from the Nazis but should we live under the Soviets? We did not know what the future held in store for us.

Just then a letter came to a friend of mine from the Army, saying that in his unit was Tana Harkavi. So I then knew that Hadaske's father was alive. My friend wrote to him about his little daughter in the orphanage. I hoped the war would end soon and Tana would come for her.

It came time for us to leave. We could not stay in Novogrudek any longer and look at the big mass graves. There were too many bad memories. We had to get away, but where? If we would not do so soon it might be too late for us. So the time for wandering for us began again.

When the war finally ended we had reached Italy. I then got a letter from Novogrudek with the very disturbing news that Tana Hakavi had been killed in the battlefield at the end of the war, without ever seeing his child.

In the meantime, a couple from Vilna came to Novogrudek to look for their relatives. As they did not find anyone, they adopted Hadaske. Eventually, they went to Israel.

In 1972 my husband and I took a trip to Israel. We visited Hadaske. What a reunion it was! We both cried a lot when I retold the whole story to her. She is a beautiful young lady, a teacher, a married woman with a nice husband and four children, all girls.

Sometimes things work out strangely, miraculously. I am very glad that I could save a Jewish orphan from being deprived of her heritage.[viii]

Hadaske, the orphan (Hadaske Harkavi, Jewish Daily Forward, March 24, 1973)

The Testimony of Murray Berger – In His Own Words

Before the War

I was born in 1912 in the town of Wseilub. Wseilub was located close to Novogrudek in what was then White Russia and is now Belorussia. Our town of Wseilub was small with only about a hundred Jewish families living there. Most of our neighbors were Gentiles—Poles and Russians. My grandfather "Leybe, the Mountain Man" lived on a high mountain in Wseilub and this was the source of the family name. He owned fields and stores and was known throughout the region as a prominent merchant. My father Avrom-Tsvi and my mother Sora were also involved in business. In some years the economics were very tough.

We were a large family. I was the youngest in a family of seven children—five brothers and two sisters. All of my brothers and sisters were married and had children. My father had four brothers and three sisters, all of who were married with children and grandchildren. On my father's side, we lost 126 family members to the Nazis.

Life was very different there than it is in America. But it was a good life for the Jews. You had to go 30 or 40 kilometers to get what you needed. People didn't have cars; they had horses and wagons. Some had a cow or two. Families had farms and stores. We stored food for the winter—radishes, potatoes, carrots, and sauerkraut. I helped out in the fields.

Wseilub boasted a range of Jewish groups and societies. Everything was soaked in Jewishness. My first language at home was Yiddish. Young people from the town traveled to study in *yeshivas*, and eventually grew into great rabbis. People went to *shul* three times a day. On *Shabbos*, you didn't do anything. You went to *shul*, came home, had *chulent* and rested. There were two rabbis in our town and many synagogues.

Jewish youth from Wseilub also set out for the great cities of Poland in the years before the war. There they were active and became members of various Jewish nationalist, secular, cultural, social and other organizations. Other young people were Zionist pioneers and set off for Israel. They were among the builders and shapers of the Jewish state.

There was plenty of Polish anti-Semitism especially in the years before the War. On Polish holidays there were anti-Semitic speakers. Jews couldn't get jobs. In the 30s, Jews were attacked in Vilna and Warsaw.

As a child, I went to Polish public schools and then to *cheder* until my bar mitzvah. When I was fourteen or fifteen my parents sent me to the famous Mirrer Yeshiva in Vilna. Vilna was known as *Yerushalayim of Lite*. They wanted me to become a rabbi. I stayed with an uncle in Vilna while I was at the *yeshiva*, but after a few years I had to leave and come home to take care of my mother, who was sick.

When the Second World War broke out, our town of Wseilub, like the entire surrounding region, was occupied by the Soviets. We hoped the times would get better. And our family, like other families, tried to stay together. But suddenly the dreadful catastrophe came.

At the end of June 1941, immediately after Hitler attacked the Soviet Union, the Germans bombed our town for a few days and after the bombings, the German Nazi hordes came in to Wseilub. A time of troubles, suffering and pain began for us and cruel decrees were issued against our *shtetl* of Jews and those of neighboring villages.

The War Begins

When the Nazis came to Wseilub, they immediately imposed a tax on the Jews. They seized my brother Zemach and me, tied us to a tree and held us as hostages to be shot in case the town didn't meet their demands. Luckily, a female doctor paid the ransom money.

Jews were driven to heavy labor camps. The Nazis or their helpers would come in the middle of the night into Jewish homes and drive out the Jews, naked, into the street, beating them murderously while robbing the homes. The Commandant of the Police, Schultz, of German origin, excelled in cruelty and avenged himself on the Jews like a good Nazi.

On Christmas Day, 1940, I saw Schultz coming towards our house with Nazi soldiers. I hid in one room as the soldiers entered another. I then jumped out of the back window and ran into a field to hide.

But there was no place to hide. All the roads and paths were filled with German army personnel in tanks and on foot. When they saw a Jew, they immediately shot him. From that day on I never again saw my *shtetl* or my family.

I decided to go to Novogrudek where maybe I could find relatives I could stay with. Through the fields and forests, back alleys and gardens, I dragged myself for miles, tired and defeated, to Novogrudek. I eventually made my way to my cousin, Alter Nochimovski, who lived on Haluwka Street. I remained there for two and a half months and endured the ordeal of the Jews of Novogrudek. While I was there, when they came looking for Jews, I hid in the attic. They took away my cousin's son who was sick in bed. He never came back.

It is impossible to describe the terrible suffering the Jews withstood at the hands of the Nazis and their local collaborators. The Jews were forced to do hard labor; they were tormented and beaten. Groups of Jews supposedly being taken to work outside the city were taken out to the fields and shot there. Jewish blood flowed like water. Right at the start, the Nazis shot 120 Jews in Novogrudek. Among them were the leading householders of the city and the members of the *intelligentsia*. Such *aktions* took place repeatedly.

On a Friday, December 5, 1941, the Nazis started to make a major *aktion*. Large pits were being dug by Jewish slave laborers behind the city near the village of Skridleve. People said that the city of Novogrudek had already been surrounded on all sides by police so that no one could escape. All of this made it clear that there would be a huge massacre, as had already happened in other towns and cities nearby. We had heard stories from people in other cities about taking Jewish people out and shooting them and we understood what was going to happen. I decided that I wasn't going to wait around to walk into the pits alive. If death had to come, let the bullet come from behind.

There was not much time for thought and I went wherever my eyes directed me. There was no one to seek advice from. I traveled by way of the forests and wanted to get closer to Wseilub. Perhaps I would meet a Jew from Wseilub who had saved himself.

I went to Shuncic, where I thought there were Jews, but nobody was there. I ran further into the forest, looking for someplace to hide. I saw a house and with my heart racing, I knocked on a door, not knowing who the owner was or whether he would hand me over to the police. But that did not happen. I asked to be allowed to warm myself and to be given something to eat. The owner, a Gentile, apprised me of the actual course of events and told me to go somewhere far off because it was not recommended to be near the city. I left immediately and went further.

I went out of the forest and saw at a distance a small farm. It did not take very long for me to make up my mind. I approached the house and knocked on the door and asked the owner if he would permit me to enter and warm up from the cold and terror of the night.

The owner permitted me to enter and allowed me to stay overnight. He provided me with something to eat, which in the bitter situation I was presently in, could not but gladden me. The farmer told me that many of the Jews of Wseilub ran to the forest with their small children to save themselves from death but the police chased them, caught several of them and led them away. A few were shot on the spot.

The next day in the morning, I heard the trucks coming to pick up the Jewish people. I ran to the forest. I heard shooting until about 2 or 3 o'clock in the afternoon even though I was on one side of the city and the shooting was on the other side. Nearly 4,000 Jews were killed in Novogrudek by the Nazis on that sorrow-laden Monday, December 8, 1941. Christians later reported that the earth was saturated with blood and the wailing and shrieking of the desperate Jews reached to the heavens. But no help came.

I wandered in the forest that whole winter, alone and suffering from cold and hunger. I pulled off the *latte*, the yellow star, from my clothing. I didn't want anybody to recognize I was Jewish. I wasn't sure if there were any Jewish people left anymore.

I wasn't dressed warm enough for the cold. Every night I knocked on a door of a Christian farmer to see if they would take pity on me and let me in to warm up, give me something to eat or to sleep overnight. The first night, I found another Christian family who knew my family from before the war. My father had a butcher store and bought cattle to slaughter from them so they remembered my family.

I never knew if they would turn me over to the Nazis or their collaborators who would shoot me.

I didn't stay too long in each place. One time a Gentile hid me in his cellar. I helped him to take care of the animals, gave them hay, cleaned the stalls and everything. One farmer hid me in the cellar overnight.

The farmers put themselves in danger, because if a Gentile was found to be hiding a Jew, he and his family would be shot and their house burned down. I hid like this the whole winter. The village police and collaborators used to come around to the villagers to get food and clothing. When I heard them coming, I had to run away to the forest. It was winter and very freezing. There was snow up to my chest. I wasn't dressed warm and sometimes I wished to finish right then and there.

One time, a farmer was hiding me and the local policemen came, so he hid me on top of an oven where he baked bread. He covered the oven so they couldn't see and I stayed there for 2-3 hours while the policemen were eating and drinking and playing cards with the farmer.

Another time, in the middle of the night during a rainstorm, I was looking for a house in which to warm up a bit and stay the night. I happened to come across a peasant hut that was situated not far from the forest. The owner was named Zibulski. He allowed me to enter to warm myself.

Before long, we heard his dog begin howling. We realized that the police, who had been searching for me, had arrived. Zibulski, his wife, and I too, became frightened. The police were there, looking expressly for me. Three policemen entered the house. I did not lose my presence of mind and immediately fled into the kitchen and from there to the exit of the house where two policemen stood guard. I approached them on a porch, sprang to the side and slipped through their hands under a hail of bullets. I ran a short stretch toward the forest and dove into a pile of snow near a shrub. I lay there until the shooting stopped.

During the very same night, I went in another direction towards a village that lay on the eastern side of Wseilub. There I went to a Christian acquaintance whose name was Fursa. He was a Russian teacher who knew my family. He helped me and related that the only Jews still alive were in the ghetto established by the Nazis in Novogrudek. I had no wish to go there because I believed that sooner or later the Jews of the ghetto would be killed. But I had no alternative.

After the massacre, the Nazis made a ghetto in Novogrudek in the Peresica section of the city. They put a wire fence all around. Five or six families had to live in one room like animals. You couldn't walk on the sidewalk; you had to walk in the middle of the street. There was big hunger because even if you had money, you couldn't go out of the ghetto to buy anything to eat.

Then the question arose as to how to enter the ghetto. The ghetto was guarded and one needed to have a yellow patch on one's clothing and to know what the best time to enter the ghetto would be. At night? During the day?

I found out that the Jews of the ghetto went out in groups under police escort twice a day to Bricianka for water because there was not enough water in the ghetto. I decided to go to Bricianka through the night in order to reach the Jews in the morning when they went out for water. And this is how it happened. I met the Jews, blended in, and after months of wandering, I entered the Novogrudek ghetto.

I wasn't dressed. I had no money. I went to the *Judenrat* to ask them for help and a place to sleep but they couldn't help me. Finally I found my sister's son Herschel who was 15 years old and living with a group of youngsters from Lida. We spoke much of the great troubles that befell our family and told one another of our difficult experiences. For my nephew and me, things were even worse than for others because we had nothing with which to purchase a piece of bread. We had to go to work in places where workers were shot while at labor. We went to work in the worst places to get a double portion of bread. My nephew Herschel was sent off with a group of workers who never returned. I never saw him again.

Suddenly one afternoon, when we were brought with a larger group of Jews to work at a sawmill on Yiddisher Street at the end of the city, the grievous news reached us that Nazi trucks filled with Lithuanians, Ukrainians, Estonians and other terrorists had come to the *shtetl* and executed a horrible slaughter in which my sister Blumka, her husband Kalman and their small sons were killed.

The clock struck six and it was time to return to the ghetto. But I decided against returning. Shlomkeh Yarmovsky was standing near me and I said to him, "Come, Shlomkeh, let's not wait. Let's go straight to the forest—we have to get away from the city if we are to have any hope of remaining alive."

Yarmovsky agreed. We jumped over the high fence that surrounded the mill and raced through the fields between stalks of corn to a small field where, exhausted, we halted and tried to catch our breath. Our first thought was, where could we hide? Meanwhile, it had started to become dark.

We heard shooting from the other side of the road that led to Nowoyelnia. The shooting took place at the barracks near Skrzydlewo where a selection was taking place—people being sent to the left or to the right. That determined who would live and who would die. We later found out that the first ones who were shot were those who had attempted to run away.

We spent the night in the forest. At the break of day, we stopped at a peasant hut and asked for something to eat. The

Christian permitted us to hide in his barn. We asked him to go to town and find out what was going on. We were told that several hundred Jews still remained alive in a smaller ghetto and were driven to work under strict guard.

We considered how we could return to the ghetto. Perhaps now, after the slaughter it would be more secure for several months. But the guard was strengthened even more and the situation became more difficult than previously.

I told Yarmovsky that we had to return to the mill and enter at night through a side field so that the guard would not hear. And so it was. Three days later, we entered the mill in the dead of night and went to the attic of the office. There we lay until the workers began to labor and then we crawled out and joined the working Jews and got back inside the ghetto.

Inside the ghetto it was very bad. People were getting beaten and shot. The Nazis kept making the ghetto smaller and smaller as they killed more Jews. I knew that soon this smaller ghetto would be liquidated also.

I decided then that I would leave the ghetto as soon as possible, before it became too late. I knew there was no existence for Jews anymore. Several young people approached me, because they knew that I was very well acquainted with the surrounding area. Our idea was to get in touch with the partisans and join them in fighting the Nazis and thus take our revenge.

In the forest

It wasn't so easy to get out of the ghetto so we had to make a plan. We were afraid of the *Judenrat* police. They hunted down people and gave the Nazis everything they wanted. If one person were missing, all would be shot.

We heard from Yehuda Bielski that his cousin, Tuvia Bielski and Tuvia's brothers Zus and Asael were in the forests and wanted to form a Jewish partisan *otriad*. A note from Tuvia to

Yehuda had been smuggled into the ghetto saying this. In August 1942, along with seven other men, we broke a ghetto fence and crawled through a large hole when a guard was not looking. We went as far as Makrec where we came to an acquaintance who linked us up with a group of three families: Chaim and Rachel Bolda and their two sons Yosef and Shlomo; Avreml Dzienciolski, his wife and their children and parents; and the Bielski brothers. I knew the Bielski family from before the war. They were from Stankiewicze, a family of eleven children, two daughters and nine sons. Soon another group of seven men escaped from the Novogrudek ghetto and joined us. We chose the Bielski brothers to head our group. Tuvia, the oldest brother, was chosen to be commander.

People from the ghetto in the group were very upset and wanted to take revenge. Our salvation lay in revenge and the desire for vengeance was great. The purpose was to harm the enemy every step of the way. As quickly as we received weaponry, we made good use of it. The group became bigger and bigger, with old and young. As it became bigger it was hard to feed a large camp of several hundred people.

We started to clean up the area to make it a safe place because Gentiles in the area used to rob the Jews of their boots, their clothes and everything. We collected food from the farmers at night. When we asked they gave it to us because they were afraid. If they didn't give, we took it by force. We said, "You have to give if you want to be alive." The people who lived there knew what was going on but were quiet because they knew the partisans would take revenge if they didn't cooperate.

Many times the Germans staged massive "searches" and we were encircled as in a trap. We ran into a big search in the Lubzchanker Forest where there were several Jewish *otriads*. In that search, the heroic commander Dr. Atlas and the commander Herschel Kaplinski both fell. An army of 80,000 Germans had taken part in that particular search. When we heard that the Germans were readying a search, we would go away deeper into the Naliboki Forest.

We did a lot of sabotage activities. Our task was to burn all the bridges on all the roads that the Germans used; tear up telephone lines which stretched from one town to the next so that no connection would be possible; blow up the rail lines which supplied the front; and other such matters of which one cannot speak of at great length.

We also sought out those policemen who served the Nazis by grabbing Jews who tried to save themselves and then handed them over to the murderers. We demolished all the places in the larger villages where the Germans wanted to establish police stations to combat the partisans. One time we heard that police were gathering in a police precinct and we took bundles of hay and put *naptha* on them and set them on fire around the precinct. We shot policemen and burned down their houses.

Once we went to Novoyelnia—a small *shtetl*—that had a railway station. The train went from Baranowice to Vilna through Lida. A large police division was stationed there. The Germans had set up a factory for dry fruits that brought them much profit. Our mission was to destroy the factory. We went in the middle of the night and accomplished it. I was the first who knocked off the guard and after me came the rest of our group. The factory was immediately put to the torch and we left with the satisfaction that our mission had succeeded.

A week later we went to ambush Germans. We started out in the middle of the night on the road running from Novogrudek to the village Waliwka where there was a big convoy of Germans.

We wanted to obtain weapons. We lay in this manner until about 11 o'clock in the morning when several trucks came by and then we fired at them. There was no doubt whatsoever that their military power outclassed ours. After an extended gunfire exchange, a truck was damaged, hit by bullets in its rubber tires.

We then lifted food from the truck and most essentially, two machine guns, four rifles and 2,500 bullets, which at that time was for us a big haul. To our great sorrow our joy was dampened when we found out that we had lost one of our comrades, H. Feldman, from Lida. It was our first loss. Later we had many more casualties.

We were in contact with Russian partisans. Sometimes we worked together. They had spies in the cities and better intelligence. Some of the Russian partisans were anti-Semitic. The Polish partisans were especially anti-Semitic. They wanted to fight Jews and many Jewish partisans died.

We were happy to fight and get revenge. When they gave me a rifle in the forest, I wished that the rifle would help me to take revenge in the name of my family and for all the Jews and that I would be able to return to the city with the rifle. My wish came true. When we got back to the city after the war, I had the same rifle with me. I gave it to a Russian.

After the War

We were in the forest for two and a half years. In 1944, the Russians pushed the Germans out and the forest was a battleground. The war was still going on in Warsaw and Lublin and the Polish were trying to free Warsaw. The Russians were fighting the Germans to Berlin. They mobilized all the partisans to come out of the forest and fight the Germans.

We knew the war was ending because we had a radio and heard that in Vitebsk, the Germans were being turned back. Groups of them were running away and came to our base and we got to fight them. In the summer of 1944 we left the forest. We lost many people on that last day before we got out of the forest. Not everybody had a rifle, but whoever did helped in the miracle of the war's end.

After we left the forest we went to the city and found out that the Russians were occupying the area. I went to Novogrudek and Wseilub but there were no Jews there, no sign of a Jewish life. Houses were empty or occupied by Gentiles. There was hunger. And that is how it was in the entire region; everything had disappeared, completely wiped out. We stayed in Novogrudek and tried to get jobs to buy things we needed. There were offices that put people to work. We worked for the city. My future wife, Fruma, was a bookkeeper for the Russian authorities.

While we were in Novogrudek we got a postcard from my older brother Ellie. He was in the Russian army and wanted to know if anybody from our family was still alive. The Russian army was waiting for the war to end and wouldn't release him, so he couldn't travel for five to six months. I got a note from a doctor that said I was very sick and sent him a telegram that said he had to come home to see me. So he got a permit to come for two to three months. We got together in Novogrudek. I had to tell him that after he escaped to Russia and was mobilized into the Russian army, his pregnant wife had given birth in the ghetto and the next day, the Nazis shot her and the baby with one bullet. Ellie did not go back to the Russian army.

We started to travel, trying to escape from Russian control. We were afraid of the Russians. The girls especially were afraid. They had to always say they had a boyfriend to protect themselves. While we were in Lublin, we found out about the *Haganah*, who worked together with the Joint Distribution Committee to help Jewish people get out of Poland. You couldn't get out because the NKVD had guards at the borders. The Israelis had agents and they bought off the border guards and organized groups of Jewish people to go through. We made up different stories to tell the guards—we're Greeks, we're from the concentration camps, we gave different names, different foreign countries.

Like this, we got through Czechoslovakia and Romania. The Joint and the *Haganah* helped us stay in Romania. They told us about synagogues and clubs. In 1945 in Romania, in a DP camp called "Kibbutz Tulda," we heard that the war was finally over. In this DP camp there were people from the ghettos and the concentration camps, many from Kovno, Lithuania. The *Haganah* was more active there. They gave us food. We were planning to go to Israel and we kept going further east to get closer to Israel. We stayed only one night in Austria on the way to Italy, but we didn't want to stay there.

In Italy, there were bigger *kibbutzim*. We were in Kibbutz Anzio, close to the sea. Fruma and I were married in Rome in the main synagogue across from the Vatican.

We tried to see what to do with the future. There were American Army reporters and we told them what happened to us. One of them said not to repeat our stories because everyone would think we were either crazy or liars. I told one of the Army reporters about my oldest brother, Harry Berger, who went to America before I was born and who was a GI in WWI. We figured out that he lived in Springfield. They told me there were many Springfields in the U.S. So they put notices in newspapers and my brother's wife Ruth saw it in the Springfield, Massachusetts paper. Harry sent us affidavits to come to the U.S. You had to have an affidavit because there were quotas. So he sponsored me, Fruma and Ellie and said he would support us if we came to the U.S. We were already in Italy for two years and we wanted to be with family, so we decided to go to the U.S.

Then we went to France to Le Havre to get on the American ship, the *Marine Flasher*. It was Pesach time and there were Chasidim on the ship and they gave us *matzah*.

We wanted to be in a place where we could live a life like every human being. We were happy to be out of Poland and in the U.S. It's a place where there's a lot to appreciate. When we came to America, first we stayed in Springfield for a few weeks.

But then we went to New York because we thought it would be easier to get work there. Albert was born and we wanted to raise a family. First we lived in furnished rooms on the Lower East Side and then in Washington Heights, East New York and Brownsville.

Life wasn't so easy. In Poland, we were surrounded by close family and it was a different life. Here, I was without a trade and without money. I had to make a living. My brother Harry wasn't rich and couldn't help us too much. I did all kinds of labor work like carpentry and construction. I tried to save up money. There were two kinds of money—*neshama gelt* for food and *kishka gelt* for the other things. Then a man brought my brother Ellie into the printing trade and later he brought me in. I was in the printers' union, Local 6, and I worked as a linotype operator for twenty years until I got my pension.

The Holocaust happened. It was *hurban shlishi*—the destruction of the third temple. I ask why God let it happen. Why didn't he make a miracle? I have no answer.[ix]

The Poems of Fruma
Gulkowich Berger

אידישע פארטיזאנער

פון פרומע גולקאװיטש-בערגער

סאמע אין דער צײט פון שװארצער יאיש־שטאנד
האט א ליכטיקער רעיון אויפגעשװדאלט : װידעראַטטאַא!
די װעלדער די געדיכטע װעלן אונזערע קאזארמעס װערן,
צו די הויכע בײמער װעלן מיר די טרײהײט שװערן.

די נאכט די פינצטערע, זי װעט אונז באשיצן,
נים קײן קאזק פון גלײכע צדדים װעלן מיר באנוצן,
נים קײן קריגער מעסטן אונזער כּוח אויס,
נאר א טויט מיט װירדע, איז אויך נצחון גרויס!

דאס הארץ איז פארטרויערט, נאר דער גוף איז מיט נחמה,
װײל דאס איז דער טאָג פון דערפילונג, די שעה פון נקמה,
אבער אויך די שעה פון דעם גורל, װאס איז נים זיכער
װאוהין עס װעט פארטראגן דער בײזער װיכער.

און אויב אזוי איז דער גורל, װײל די װעלט האט אונז פאראטן
װעלן מיר דא מוטיג קעמפן מיטן ביקם און מים גראנאטן!
מעג די ליכטיקע פאדריגיען, שאטנס פארן אײג זיך שװארצן
הײנט מײן חבר איז געפאלן, עס איז אן אומעט אויפן הארצן.

װײל עס איז נים קײן קאזק פון גלײכן און נים פון יושר אויכעט,
נאר א קאמף פון לעמל, װאם האט זיך געשטעלט געגן שוחט,
אבער לעמל איז פלוצינג פארװאנדלט געװאָרן אין לײבן
מיט נאאגעם אין די הענט — אין א בעסערן מארגן מיר גלױבן!

די שעה האט געשלאגן, די צײם איז געקומען
א רוף : גײן אין קאמף — דעם ביקם שנעל גענומען
מיט אש פון חרוגים דער הײנם האם געטריבן,
מים בלוט פון מיליאנען מײן מום איז פארשריבן.

א שאם האם געהילכט — איך בין אויף דער װאך,
נקמה עם רופם ! איך בין גרייט פאר דער זאך.
איך װײס, אז מײן קאמף, א גערעכטער : איך פיל —
צו פארניכטן דעם שונא, דאס איז מײן ציל.

אין לאַגער אַ טומעל, מען כאַפּט דאָס געוװער,
עס לויפֿן די קולן אַהין און אַהער,
מיט ערנסטער פֿרומקייט, װי צו הייליקער תּפֿילה־
פֿירט מען אַ קאַמף, װאָס מען רופֿט איצט „געװילע"

עס פֿאַלט שוין די נאַכט זו, מען צײלט דעם פֿאַרלוסט,
פֿאַרװאָס גרייט צו שטאַרבן האָט יעדער געװאוסט !
איבער װי־עלדער געריכטבע, װיימער אױך שפֿאַן
מיטן ביקס אױפֿן אַקסל אין האַנט דעם נאַגאַן.

אין שעה פֿון באַפֿרייאונג איך שטײ װי אַ שומר,
מיר דאַכט אױף מײן זיכן עס װיינען די בײמער,
עס איז מײן געזיכט נאָך מיט אומגליק באַפֿאַרבן,
עס מאָנט יעדער שטײן און עס שרײט יעדער קרבן ! ...

JEWISH PARTISANS

At the very time of black despair's grim chance
A brilliant thought shone forth: resistance!
The dense forests into barracks changed will be,
And to the lofty trees we'll swear our loyalty.

The gloomy night will our protector be,
It's not strife of equal partners that we'll see,
Not warriors here shall our power mete,
But death with dignity is also triumph great!

The heart is sad but the body is with comfort filled,
For 'tis the day when vengeance's hour will be fulfilled.
Also the hour of fate, uncertain I must say,
Whither the angry storm our lives will bear away.

And if this is our fate, since the world has us betrayed,
With courage shall we fight, with gun and with grenade!
The bright days pass, 'fore me dark shadows rise,
My comrade fell today, gloom grips me in its vise.

For it is not a struggle of equals, justice fair,
But against the slaughterer a lamb's struggle in despair,
Yet suddenly lamb as lion transformed we see
Fight with pistol in its hands for a better morning, free!

The hour has struck, 'tis time to take a stand.
A call to battle! Quickly take the gun in hand!
The ash of murdered ones the wind has blown,
With blood of millions is my courage sown.

I stand here on guard—a shot rends the air,
For vengeance it calls! For the mission I bear.
My struggle is just, this in my soul I feel,
The enemy to destroy – that is my goal.

The camp is aroused, to their arms they go,
The bullets are flying to and fro,
With earnest piety, sacred as prayer,
To strife called "guerrilla" into battle we dare.

The night is descending, take stock of the dead,
Death stalks our path, but for this we're prepared!
Over dense forests now onward I bend,
With gun at my shoulder, with pistol in hand.

I stand like a guard at the hour I'm free,
At my sigh the trees seem to mourn with me,
Lines of misfortune still etched in my face,
Stone and victim cry out, the loss to replace!

I can still feel the tremor, the horror, the rage
Through blood-soaked whips of my holocaust-age,
From mountains of corpses goes my wandering soul,
With gun on my shoulder through dense forests I roam.

Sole survivor am I, no place need I hasten,
For miles and miles death its grim toll has taken....
Victory,... how can I with triumphant tread
Join the nations that march, while I mourn for these dead?

Many an image appears 'fore my eyes,
Time like an arrow from its bow can fly,
But forget shall I never that season's black day
Of blood and of flame that has shadowed my way.

THE YOUNG MOTHER

Like a misty wind on a summer's night
The mother took the dead child to the dark forest
She shakes a little
and hardly managed to rest on something
And what she rested on, a tree, she did not care.

The night, a black one,
covered everything
But the sparks of madness in her look
Moved her feet.

The mother walks from far away, mile after mile
Since her mind was emptied
Her body, her heart, her child, a little one
Today had tasted the first spoonful of tea.

She hugs the little body, she searches,
She touches where it is sore,
And why is the diaper not wet?
Suddenly the mother's madness imagines
everything about her is crying
And she batters her head against the tree.

She saw it, everything in front of her eyes
Her house..... It burns!
A German runs to her,
He grabs the child and throws her down
And it scorches her very being.

And further, further, the head could not take it anymore
Who is crying, the child?
It wants to eat?
Wait! She bends down quickly
the milk in the full breast is painful.

She bares her breasts. Here, suck, she begs
The breast remains bare and the wind cools and fondles it
The mother thinks it is the mouth,
The little hands of her child.

The skies light up, a ray shines
And partisans arrive and gaze at the scene:
The dead child, the young woman,
the breasts in the blue hands of the child.
With pain and tears, they recognize a friend.

1941

פֿון פֿרומע גולקאָװיטש - בערגער

יאָר ניינצן פֿערציג איינס,
די זון איז שװאַרץ — לבנה, רויט —
געשטען איז עם אַזוינס
הערן אויף מיין לאַנד
עם האָט געהערשט היטלער-שלאַנג.
בייט און שאַנד
עם האָט צעטיילט צװישן זיך,
דעם צייטן-גאַנג.
שטיבער ביי די װעגן ברענען
די שװאַרצע נאַבט שפּיגלט זיך
אין רויטע פֿלאַמען
און קאָן אַליין זיך ניט דערקענען.
װייל בלוט און פֿלאַם
עם שטאַנט בוזאַמע.
אין דעם אַש פֿון זעקס מיליאָן
פֿאַרברענט מענטשן-דרעכט.
קוקט אַרויס דאָם רעכט
פֿון אומשענסט װאָם,
געבריעם האָט און געשעכט,
װאָם מיט בלבול און שפֿאָט.
שװאַרץ געמאַכט דעם קלאַנג,
װאָם מיט אידיש בלוט ער האָט
געשטילט זיין הייה'שן פֿאַרלאַנג ! ...

אַן אויף אַ בוים אין בלעטער קרוינען
זינגם הויך דער סאָלאָוועי,
זײַן ליד װיל אין די רוימען
איבערשרײַען שאַנד און װײ...
עס הויבן יונגע האַזן
אין זעלדל פֿאַלט דאָס װאַסער,
עס מײַנען זיך די גראָזן
בײַ פֿאַרדעקן עפּעס — מאַכן בלאַסער.
קענען בלאַסער װערן
די בריזנעעדיגע אויוואָנם?
קען די גראָז פֿאַרדעקן
די ערד װאָס האָט געהויבן?
קען פֿון מיליאָנען פֿײַן און װײ
איבערשרײַען דער סאָלאָװעי?
און אין זעלדל בלײַבן קװאַלן
שטראָמען, זיהן װען עס פֿאַלן...
פֿון הײַקן פֿון צעברענטע גופֿים
װערם די זון שװאַרץ װי בראַנד
און די לבֿנה, רויט פֿון שאַנד.

1941

The year – nineteen forty-one.
The sun is black, the moon is red.

It came to pass
when my country
was ruled by the Hitler-snake.
Death and humiliation
divided the passage of time between themselves.
Houses by the road are burning.
The black night looks at its reflection
in red flames,
and cannot recognize itself,
because death and flames are together on the march.

In the ashes of six million burnt-up human rights,
becomes apparent what is deserved
by the inhuman,
who burned and slaughtered,
who with slander and derision,
obliterated the reports
of how he sated his bestial lust
with Jewish blood.

And on a tree in crowns of leaves
The nightingale sings loudly.
The sound of his song wants to
drown out humiliation and suffering.
Young hares are running,
in the forest the water is falling.
The grass is making every effort
to cover something up – to make it paler.

Can the burning ovens
ever be made paler?
Can grass cover
the earth that was heaving?
Can the pain and suffering of millions
be drowned out by a nightingale?

And in the woods, blood is streaming.
From the smoke of burnt bodies
The sun becomes as black as charcoal
And the moon, red with shame.

די לעצטע ביז איך

פון פרומע גולקאָוויטש - בערגער

די לעצטע צו געדענקען, געבליבן בין איך,
די געדאַנקען ביי דער נאַכט, עס מאַטערן מיך.
עס גליען די פייערן פון דעם גרויסן ציפער,
דער הויטאַג אין האַרצן, עס ווערט אַלץ טיפער.

אַט שוועבן אויף פאַר מיר, ווי פריש די גריבער,
דער שוידער פון די אומגעבראַכטע שוועסטער, ברידער.
די ערד האָט גערוקוערט, דער אַרום האָט געשוויגן,
און די קליינע קינדערלעך, — אַ ציפער נאָר געבליבן.

איך קוק אויף צוריק, איך זע יענעם טאָג, יענע שעה,
אַזוי הערלעך שיין, נאָר פלוצלינג, — מלחמה איז דאָ !
באַלד מאַכט זיך אין שטעטל אַ רעש,
איינער לויפט, דער צווייטער וויינט, און מען פאַקט באַגאַזש.

קוים דורכגעלעבט די פינצטערע אָן שרעקעוודיגע נאַכט,
ס׳קומט שוין אָן דער טאָג, דער טרײבער, מיט אַ נייע מאַכט.
אַ מאַכט פון רשעים, אַ מאַכט פון גזלנים,
און דאָס גאַנצע שטעטל האָט שוין אַן אַנדער פנים.

די אידן, מען טרײבט זיי פון זייערע היימען אַרויס,
די גויים, אונזערע שכנים, זיי טאַנצן פאַראויס.
זיי נעמען פון אונז אַוועק גוטס און האָב,
און שפיען אין פנים און באַלײדיגן גראָב.

און אַט זיינען שוין דאָ די געשטאַפאָ, מיט אַ באַפעל,
די אידן מוזן אָנטאָן אַ לאַטע, זאָל זיין געל.
יעדער טאָג, אַ נייע גזירה פון די עסיעסן,
קאָן מען דען דעם ,,ספעקטאַקל״ פאַרגעסן ?

With Courage Shall We Fight

ווען מען האָט אַלטער סרעברעניק אויף אַ שטריק געפירט,
זוי אַ הונט געטריבן, דורך אַלע גאַסן „מאַרשירט".
איך קאָן ניט פאַרגעסן דעם שרעקלעכן מאָמענט,
ווען עס האָבן זיך דערהערט קולות — עס ברענט !

די הייליגע ספרים, — די ספרי-תורות, — אין פלאַמען,
צוויי בעזשענצעס, אין אָרון קודש, געשאַסן צוזאַמען.
אַט שטייען שוין אַלע אויפ׳ן מאַרק אין רייען,
פאַרטריבן פון שטעטל — צום לעצטן „מאַרש" — מיר גייען.

די לעצטע בין איך צו געדענקען, ווּ עס איז געווען מיין הויז,
די מענטשן צו וועמען מיין ליבשאַפט איז גרוים.
ווּאו זיינען די שוועסטער, די ברידער, די פריינט ?
ווּאו זיינען מיין מאַמע און טאַטע היינט ? ...

I AM THE LAST

I am the only one left to remember.
My thoughts torment me at night.
The fires of the huge number blaze
as the anguish in my heart
grows deeper and deeper.

Drifting before me:
how fresh the graves are!
The terror of my murdered
brothers and sisters.
Smoke rising from the earth.
Now silence all around.
And nothing is left of the little children
but a number.

I look back and see that day, that hour,
So majestically beautiful.
And suddenly there's war!
Disorder erupts in the town.
This one runs. That one weeps.
Everyone is packing to go.

We have barely made it through
the terrifying dark night
when a new day breaks, uncaring,
under a new command.
Domination by villains, a regime of robbers.
And the town has utterly mutated.

The Jews are driven out of their homes.
The Gentiles, our neighbors,
dance with anticipation.
They seize all of our belongings
and pay us with spit in our faces,
obscenely insulting us.

And before you know it the Gestapo is there,
with their edict:
"You must wear a yellow patch"
Every day, some new decree from the SS.

Can this "performance" be forgotten?
When they led Alter Strebrenik by a rope,
dragged him like a dog,
and "marched" him through the streets.

I cannot forget that horrifying moment
When the screams of "FIRE!" reached us.
The holy books, the Torah scrolls, in flames.
Two grenades thrown into the Aron Kodesh at once.

Now, all of us are standing in rows
in the marketplace.
Driven from the town,
we set off on our final march.

I am the last to remember
where my house was,
the last to remember those I loved so well.
Where are my sisters, my brothers, my friends?
Where are my mother and father today?

ברויט און געטאָ

פֿון פֿרומע גולקאָוויטש-בערגער

פֿאַרוואָס איז דאָס אַזוי, זאָג מיר. וועלט —
אַז אַ שטיקל ברויט זאָל זיין טייערער פֿון געלט?
אַ פֿענעצל ברויט צו שטילן דעם הונגער
אַ לעבעלע ברויט וואָס מען קוקט ווי אויף וואָנדער.

ברויט, ברויט, עס הונגערט מיך אַזוי — ביים האַרצן, עס נאָגט,
הער איך ווי דאָס קליין מיידעלע, צו איר מאַמען זאָגט.
אוי, מיין קינד, אין געטאָ איז ניטאָ קיין ברויט צום עסן,
מאָרגן אפֿשר וועט זיין בעסער — דערווייל איז צו פֿאַרגעסן.

אָ, ברויט! היינט ביסטו מיין טרוים, און דער ציל פֿון לעבן,
אַ שטיקל ברויט צו זאַט עסן, דאָס איז מיין שטרעבן.
און איינמאָל, ווען דער טאָג איז געווען ניט אַזוי העל,
האָט מיך באַגליקט צו קריגן אַ ביסל מעל.

אָבער דורכטראַגן דעם יעקל, אַז דער פּאָליציאַנט זאָל ניט זען,
איז דאָס ניט צו באַגרייפֿן, וואָס פֿאַראַ מסירת נפֿש דאָס איז געווען.
ווייל פֿאַר אַ קאַרטאָפֿל האָט שוין ניט איינער באַצאָלט מיט׳ן לעבן,
איז וואָס פֿאַראַ שטראָף וואָלטן די רוצחים פֿאַר׳ן ברויט געגעבן?

עס איז מיין טאָג געווען — דער זשאַנדערמאַן האָט פֿאַרקוקט,
מיין טאַטע, ביי דער נאָרע, נאָך אַ קאַפּיטל תהילים, ער זאָגט.
די שוועסטער זיי האָבן שוין צוגעגרייט דאָס דייזשעע,
ווער האָט גאָר געטראַפֿט, אַז עס קומט שוין אָן די שעה, די בייזע.

אַ אויווען מען היצט, די מעל איז שוין פֿאַרשאָטן,
אין דייזשעע, עס וואַקסמט, עס ווואַקסמט, דער ברויט איז פֿאַרקנאָטן,
אָבער פּלוצלינג דערהערט זיך פֿון דרויסן אַ יאָמערי, אַ געשריי,
דער געטאָ איז שוין אַרומגערינגלט, מיט מערדער אוי, ווײ!

די פֿלאַמען אין אויווען, זיי לעשן שוין אויס,
די טייג, שפּאַרט פֿון דייזשעע, פֿון אויבן אַרויס,
ניטאָ שוין קיין הענט צו באַקן דעם ברויט,
עס ליגן שוין אַלע אין פֿערעסיקער גריבער, טויט! . . .

און פֿאַר׳יתזום׳ט איז די דייזשעע ברויט אויפֿ׳ן נאָרע געבליבן,
פּונקט ווי עס האָט געפֿילמט, אַז אויך איר האָט מען באַטריבן.
טאָ זאָג מיר וועלט, ווי קענסטו מיין צער זען?
חרוב געמאַכט מיין פֿאָלק! זאָג וואָס איז מיט דיר געשען?

BREAD IN THE GHETTO

Why is it so – tell me, World,
That a morsel of bread is worth more than gold?
A slice of bread to quiet the hunger
A loaf of bread, looked upon as a wonder.

"Bread, bread, I am so hungry – it's gnawing my heart away"
I hear the little girl to her mother say.
"Oh, my child, in the ghetto there is no bread to eat.
Tomorrow will perhaps be better – meanwhile we must forget, my sweet."

Ah, bread! Today you are the dream that stokes my life's fire.
A piece of bread to eat – my dearest desire.
Once, before day's dawning hour,
I managed to get hold of a little flour.
But carrying the sack so that the policeman might not see –
You cannot fathom what sacrifice that required of me!
For a potato, more than one smuggler lay dead!
What punishment would the murderers mete out for bread?

It was my day, the policeman looked away!
My father is standing with his Psalms, to pray.
My sisters are waiting, the kneading trough prepared,
We couldn't imagine the approaching hour when no one would be spared.

The dough already kneaded, the oven getting warm,
Rising in the trough, the loaves about to form.
But suddenly pleading and screaming reach our ears,
The ghetto is surrounded by murderers – the worst of our fears.

The flames in the oven are but barely glowing,
From trough and from oven, the dough is overflowing.
There are no more hands to bake the bread
In their pitiless graves lies everyone – dead.

The bread in the trough, abandoned on the sideboard it stands,
As inevitable as its overflow, our delivery into "their" hands.
So tell me, world, can you feel this pain as I do?
You destroyed my people. Tell me: What happened to you?

איך געדענק!

פון פרומע גולקאָוויטש-בערגער

עם טראָגן זיך ווי בליצן פון גרויזאַמען שטורעם
די געדאַנקען וואָס ברענגען צוריק די יסורים,
עם גייען מיר פאַרביי מיט פיין און שוידער אַלטן
אַזויפיל פאַר'יאוש'טע, פאַרבלוטיגטע געשטאַלטן.

איך געדענק, די פנימ'ער פון רוצחים, פון קרבנות,
און פייער-פלאַמען אין נעכט פון לבנות,
אַ נאַצי-שלאַנג האָט אָנגעצונדן שריפה
שטאָט, נאָך שטאָט, געשפרייט האָט זיך מגפה.

הינטער געטאָ־וואַנט געשריבן אַלט און יונג און קינד,
נאָר דער נאָמען ,,איד" איז געווען די זינד,
ריי נאָך ריי אויף לעצטן וועג מען שפּאַנט —
געטריבן אונטער ביקס און מערדערישע האַנט.

געפּייניגט! מיט שנאה, האָם ביז טויט,
פאַרווייסט אַלק, וואָם יאָרן לאַנג געבויט,
אין די מונדירן מיט די האַקנקרייץ מעדאַלן,
זיי שמייכלען, און שלאָגן, שיסן און שאַלן.

אָט זע איך איצט דעם האַקנקרייץ מיט די פינצטערערע שלייפן,
און העלזער פון ליכטיגע מיידלעך די שלייפן פאַרציען...
געקוקט, און געקוואַלן האַבן די מערדער, די באַנדיטן,
ווי אידיש בלוט רינט, ווי דאָס גרוב הויבט זיך אין מיטן.

אין די גאָז־קאַמערן דערשטיקט, געוואָרפן אין די פייער־צונגען,
פאַרשניטן מיין דור, — מיליאָנען פאַרשלונגען!
אין פאַרשטומטן געשריי וועץ מויל איז שוין פאַרברענט,
שרייען נאָך מיליאָנען אויסגעשטרעקטע הענט...

און ווען מען האָט דאָס שלעכטם דערקענט,
עם האָט אין יוגנט אויפגעברענט, —
נקמה ! עם רופט צום גרויסן העלדן־שטרייט,
די שונאים צו פֿאַרניכטן, עם קלינגט פֿון נאָענט און ווייט.

און מוטיג זיינען אויפגעשטאַנען העלדן
אין געטאָס, לאָגערן, וואַלד און פֿעלדן,
מיט ביקס, נאַגאַן, גראַנאַט אין האַנט,
צום אומגלייכן קאַמף געשטעלט זיך, ביי געטאַ־וואַנט.

עם שטרייכט און פֿעכט, מיט שטאָלצן מוט,
פֿאַר כבוד'פֿון אַ פֿאָלק ! פֿאַר מאַרטירער־בלוט !
עם הילכט אַ קרעכץ, געפֿאַלן איז אַ העלד,
און ליגט פֿאַרוואונדעט־טויט, אין געטאָ, וואַלד און פֿעלד.

וואו עם האָט געפֿלאַקערט היים דער שטרייט,
געפֿאַלן זיינען העלדן, — זייער בלוט עם מאָנט, עם שרייט.
הייליג אייער אָנדענק ! שטאָלץ איז אייער מוט !
אויף אייביג איז פֿאַרשריבן, אייער העלדן־טויט מיט בלוט !

I REMEMBER

They come upon me like lightning bolts in a fierce storm -
The thoughts that bring back the agony,
So many hopeless, bloody images
Pass before me with old pain, old horror, old revulsion.

I remember the faces of the murderers and their victims,
And fiery flames on moonlit nights,
A Nazi serpent started the inferno.
In city after city, the fire spread.

Behind the ghetto wall were old, and young, and infants.
Their only sin was to have the name "Jew."
Column after column were marched to their end,
Driven by rifles and the murderer's hand.

Tortured! With hatred, mortal hatred,
Everything we built, over long years, was destroyed.
In their uniforms with the swastika medals,
They smile, and batter, and shoot, and exult over their "accomplishments."

Now again I see the swastikas. And the sinister nooses,
That deformed the throats of radiant young girls.
Those murderers, those criminals watched and beamed with pride
As Jewish blood flowed, and the mass graves piled high.

Suffocated in the gas chambers, and thrust into the fire,
My generation was cut down.
Millions were consumed.
In silenced protestation–when their mouths were already burnt up -
Countless still screamed with outstretched hands.

And when the evil had been recognized,
It flared up within the young:
Revenge! The call to a great, heroic battle
To destroy our enemies rang out near and far.

Courageously, heroes rose up
In ghettoes, camps, forests, and fields
With rifles, pistols, and grenades in hand
And entered into an unequal struggle near the ghetto wall.

They battled and they fought with proud courage
For the dignity of their people and the martyrs' blood.
A sigh resounds. A hero has fallen,
And lies, mortally wounded, in ghetto, forest, or field.

Wherever the battle raged,
Heroes fell. Their blood makes demands. It cries out:
"Your memory is holy. Your courage is a source of pride."
Their deaths forever inscribed with the blood they spent.

אויפשטאַנד אין וואַרשעווער געטאָ

פון פרומע גולקאָװיטש - בערגער

יאָר נײַנצן פערציג דרײַ
מאָנאַט אַפּריל, באַלד שױן מאַי
געקומען איז דער פרילינג דער ליבער
יוב - פסח איז דעם שװעל אַריבער.

מיט שרעק אין בליק האָבן אידישע קינדער
געשלונגען די אכזריות פון נאַצי אַצינדער
„עבדים הײַנו", האָט הױך דאָ געקלונגען
גענוג שױן דאָס בראױט פון קנעכטשאַפט צו שלינגען

עס שװעבן פאַר די אױגן מיט אומרו נײעם
די בלוטיגע צײַטן פון אַלטן מצרים,
נאָר עס קומט ניט קײן נביא, עס קומט ניט קײן רעטער
צום אױפשטאַנד אַ רוף, געהילכט האָט אין געטאָ.

שװאַרק איז דער הימל, עס שלענגלען זיך בליצן
װי פון בײזע װאָלקינס, טוען פײער שפּריצן,
צום סדר צום ערשטן, עס האָט װי אַ שטורעם
אױף גאַס פון דער געטאָ צעטראָגן די בשורה.

עס טרײסלען זיך די װענט און די הימלען זיך הױדען
מען שיסט אױפ'ן געטאָ, און מען ענטפערט פון בױדעם,
די װאַרשעװער העלדן פון װעלט מאַרטירער-פאָלק
מיט אומדערשראָקן גבורה קעמפן געגן נאַצי - פאָלק!

מיט גראָנאַטן, מיט ברענענדיגע פלעשער דעם כבוד זיי באַשיצן
הײליגער צאָרן פון זייערע אױגן שפּריצן,
אױף שנאה מיט שנאה, אױף פײער מיט פײער
געשטעלט זיך גענן טױט, פאַר אַ װעלט אַ פרײַער!

איבער װייסל-ברעג טראָגט זיך אַ פלאַמיגער שײַטער
איבער געטאָ חורבן שפּאַנט אַלץ גרעסער, אַלץ װײַטער,
דורך רױכן קנױלן, אױף געטאָ װאַנט —
דער לעצטער חלוץ שפּאַנט...

מיט װײַס-בלױע פאָן, מיט שװערד מיט בלױזן
שיצט ער די לעצטע װאַך, פון שולן פון קלױזן.
אין טאָגיגן באַגינען, אין יאַמערדיגן געדרענג
דער לעצטער אױסגעשרײַ: „פאַר אונזער בלוט ניט שווײגט"!

With Courage Shall We Fight

מיט װײַס־בלױע פֿאָן, מיט שװערד מיט בלײַזן
שיצט ער די לעצטע װאַך, פֿון שולן פֿון קלױזן.
אין מאָגיגן באַגינען, אין יאָמערדיגן געדרענג
דער לעצטער אויסגעשרײַ: „פֿאַר אונזער בלוט ניט שענק"!

באַמבע־פֿלאַם אויף מענטש און שטיבער
פֿאַרװאַנדלט האָט דעם געטאָ אין װיסטע גריבער.
עס איז אַ יסורים, העלדנטויט מגילה
װאָס מיט בלוט און פֿײַער איז געמאָלן די הילע.

פֿינף־און־צװאַנציג יאָר שוין פֿאַרבײַ
פֿון חורבן עם קריכן די שאָטנס ארויס אויף דער פֿרײַ
דערשטיקט, צעקאַליעטשעט, פֿאַר'סמ'ט און פֿאַרברענט
און מאָנען: געדענק, פֿאַר אונזער בלוט ניט שענק!"

UPRISING IN THE WARSAW GHETTO

1943 –
The month of April. Almost May.
The beloved Spring has come.
And Passover has crossed the threshold.

With terror in their faces, Jewish children
Swallowed the Nazis' brutality.
"Slaves we have already been" rang out loud.
"We've swallowed enough of the bread of slavery!"

It floats before their eyes with new anxiety,
The bloody era in ancient Egypt.
But neither prophet nor savior now comes.
A call to rise up is sounded in the ghetto.

Black is the night sky with streaks of lightning.
Fire sprays down, as if from furious clouds.
A flash of news came to the Seder,
Like a storm on the street of the ghetto.

The walls tremble and the skies shake.
The ghetto is being shot at, and Jews return fire from the roofs.
The heroes of Warsaw, from the world's martyr-nation,
With fearless strength are battling against the Nazi regiment!

With grenades, with burning bottles, they guard their honor.
Holy wrath bursts from their eyes,
Hate for hate, fire for fire
Standing up against death, for a free world!

With Courage Shall We Fight

Along the Vistula's banks, a flaming torch is carried,
Over the destroyed ghetto, with ever greater and wider strides,
Through billows of smoke, on top the ghetto wall,
Walks the last brave soul.

With white-blue flag, with sword –
He keeps the final vigil, from schools and synagogues.
At the beginning of day, with solemn insistence,
The final cry: "There is no pardon for shedding our blood!"

Flaming bombs on people and houses
Transformed the ghetto into desolate pits.
It is an epic tale of suffering and of heroes' deaths,
Whose cover is illustrated with pictures drawn with blood and fire.

Twenty-five years have already passed,
From the destruction, shadows are crawling free.
Strangled, crippled, poisoned, and burnt
And they demand: "Remember, there is no pardon for shedding
our blood!"

יאָרצייט ליכט

פון פרומע גולקאָוויטש - בערגער

איך קוק נאָך די צייט, אין די שוואַרצע לוחות,
ווען איך צינד אָן נאָך די מאַרטירער, יאָרצייט ליכט,
זע איך, דעם טייוול פון די בייזע רוחות,
וואָס ס'האָט מיין פֿאָלק געשעכט און פאַרניכט.

דאָס ערשטע ליכט צינד איך נאָך דיר, מיין מאַמע,
פאַרברוביבן ביסטו אין דיין קבר אַ איינזאַמע,
פינצטמער, פראָסטיג, איז געווען דער פיין,
ווען דו האָסט אויסגעהויכט די נשמה דיין.

דיין איינציג זון האָט געמוזט דיין קבר מאַכן גרייט,
אָבער אַלע קינדער האָבן דיר צו אייביגקייט באַגלייט,
קאַטש אַלעמען האָט געשטיקט די זעלבע ווי און טרערן,
האָט מען דיין טויט מקנא געווען, דעם שווערן.

איצט נאָך דעם גרויסן חורבן פון זעקס מיליאָנען,
עס טוליען נאָך די פייערן, וואָס ווענקן, וואָס מאָנען,
פרעג איך אייך, מענטשהייט : וויפיל ליכט זאָל איך צינדן ?
מיין אויסגעמאַטערט מוח קאָן גאָר ניט באַגרינדן.

ווען אין די געדאַנקען קומען אונטער די לעצטע חשבונות,
אַזעלכע פאַרצווייגטע משפחות געווען פון יוגנט און זקנות ..
עס ברענען זעקס יאָרצייט-ליכט פאַר אַלע צוזאַמען —
פאַר ברידער און שוועסטער, פאַר טאַטן און מאַמען.

אין נעפל אין שוואַרבן, טויכן אויף געשטאַלטן,
פון גרווילעכן אומרעכט, וואָס די וועלט האָט באַהאַלטן,
אַזוי פיל דאַ אומגליק אין איטליכן שאָטן,
דאָס בלוט רינט נאָך, און מאָנט, אין שטומקייט פאַרקנאָטן.

ווען זיי קאָנען דערצײַלן, ווען זיי קאָנען זאָגן,
די פלאַמען פון די ליכט, דעם טרויער, וואָס טראָגן,
די וועלט עס זאָל הערן, די וועלט עס זאָל געדענקען
ניט צו דערלאָזן, עס זאָל אויפשטיין אַ העננקער.

YAHRTZEIT CANDLES

I look up the dates in calendars of black days past.
And when I light memorial candles for the martyrs
I see the demon of evil spirits
who slaughtered and annihilated my people.

The first candle, I light for you, my mother.
You remained alone in your grave, among the first.
The suffering was dark and cold
when your soul expired.

Your only son had to prepare your grave,
But all of your children accompanied you to eternity.
Although everyone stifled their grief and tears,
They envied your early death.

Now, after the great destruction of six million,
The fires still glow under the ashes, provoking, demanding.
I ask you, Mankind: "How many candles should I light?"
My exhausted brain cannot conceive it.

When the final calculations come into my thoughts,
There were such large extended families, young and old...
There are six candles burning – for everyone, together.
For brothers and sisters, for fathers and mothers.

In the dark fog, images surface
Of the outrageous injustice that the world had hidden.
So much tragedy in every shadow,
The blood is still flowing,
Its demands interwoven with "muteness."

If they could recount, if they could speak—
The flames of the candles that bear the sorrow—
The world should take notice, and remember,
Never to allow another executioner to rise.

תהילים-זאַנגער

פֿון פֿרומע גולקאָװיטש-בערגער

די נאַכם פֿאַרגייט, עס נעמט שוין טאָגן
איך הער מײן טאַטן תהילים זאָגן,
פֿרום, געלײטערט פֿון דוד׳ס לידער,
אין שול צום דאַװנען ער לויפֿט שוין װידער.

אַרום בית-מדרש שטײען רעדלאַך אידן
אַלע רײדן װעגן „נאַצי", װעגן מלחמה און פֿריִדן,
עס װינטיגט דעם אַפּעטיט זאַבעדיגער װעג-שטום
און דער נאַצי-מערדער לויערט שוין אומעטום.

אין שרעקעהודיגע, זינגענדיגע שטיבלאַך —
אײנגעהילט אין טלית און תפֿילין
אידן זאָגן תהילים —
אַלע האָבן אײן פֿאַרלאַנג, אײן געבעט :
גאָט, שיק די הילף ניט צו שפּעט !

און צװישן זײ מײן טאַטע טוט זײן תפֿילח
פֿאַר זײן הויזגעזינד, פֿאַר דער גאַנצער הײליגער קהילה,
גאָט, דערבאַרעמדיגער : מײן געבעט טו דערהערן,
װאוהין זיך צו װענדן ? װאוהין זיך צו קערן ?

אַ עדה אידן אין טרויער, אין יאָמער, אין צער
שרײיען צום רבוני של עולם : טו אפּ דעם גזר !
שטערקן די העגט צו די הימלען פֿון די פֿײער-צונגען
נאָר די װאָלקנס די געדיכטע דעם געבעט האָבן פֿאַרשלונגען,

אַ גליִַנדיגער ציגל אַציִנד די זון צװישן רויכן קנויִלן
ניטאָ מער קײן תהילים-זאַנגער אין די שטעטלאַך אין פֿױלן,
צו זינגען דוד׳ס לידער פֿון לויבן,
צו מורמלען װערטער פֿון טרײיסט און פֿון גלויבן.

THE RECITER OF PSALMS

The night is passing – day is starting to break.
I hear my father reciting Psalms,
Pious, purified by David's songs,
He's running to the synagogue to pray yet again.

Around the shul stand circles of Jews
All of them are talking about "Nazis,"
about war, and freedoms lost.
The wind is blowing on the open, sandy road – noiselessly
And the Nazi murderer lurks everywhere in wait.

In prayer-rooms filled with terror and singing,
Wrapped in *tallis* and *tefilin*,
Jews are reciting Psalms.
All have but one request, one prayer
"God, send your help before it is too late!"

One among them, my father, with his prayer
For his household and for the entire holy congregation:
"Merciful God, hear my prayer. Where can we turn?
Which direction should we go?"

A group of Jews – in mourning, in misery, in pain
Call to the Master of the Universe: "Annul this decree!"
They reach their hands up toward the heavens
from the tongues of fire,
But the thick clouds swallow their prayers.

The sun is now a glowing hot brick
among billows of smoke.
There are no more Psalm-sayers
in the small towns of Poland
To sing David's songs of praise,
To mumble words of consolation and faith.

אידישע קינדער אין דער היטלער-עפּאָכע

פֿון פֿרומע גולקאָוויטש-בערגער

היטלען בלויע, גרינע גראָזן
קינדער שפּרינגען ווי די האָזן,
טאַנצן, פֿרייען זיך מיט גאַט'ס וועלט
און מען שפּילט זיך אין באַהעלטל.

היטלען שוואַרצע — ווינטן וויעען
געקומען איז דער נאַצי געטאָס בייען
קינדער הונגערן — קינדער וויינען
קיינער וויל קיין הילף ניט ברענגען

היטלען גרויע — רויכערן קנוילן
קינדער שיקט מען מיט ביקסן קוילן
קינדער וואַרפֿט מען אין פֿייערצבונגען
ווער האָט יושר פֿון וועלט פֿאַרשטוילנגען ?

שטראָמען בלוטן — טייכן טרערן,
פֿון שרעק די היטלען בלאַס זיי ווערן.
שבואר אין פֿינצטער איז די נאַכט
אויף דער וועלט פֿון היטלער'ס מאַכט.

ניטאָ מער קינדער האָס שפּילן און רוישן
נאָר רייגיע קבֿרים פֿון הייליגע קדושים,
ניטאָ מער קיין קינדער צו זינגען אַ ליד
אין דער לאַנד וואו געשטאָטען איז מיין וויג.

ווי זינגען איצט פֿייגל איבער יענער ערד ?
ווי וואָקסן בלוטמען מיט קינדערבלוט גענערט ;
ווי שיינט די זון מיט גאָלדענע שטראַלן ?
ווען אַ מיליאָן אידישע קינדער — זיינען געפֿאַלן ? ...

JEWISH CHILDREN IN THE HITLER ERA

Skies of blue, grass of green
Children are jumping like hares,
Dancing, enjoying God's little world,
Playing hide-and-seek.

Black clouds – winds howl.
The Nazi has come to build ghettos.
Children are starving – children are crying.
No one wants to offer any aid.

Skies of gray – billows of smoke
Children are shot with rifle bullets.
Children are thrown into tongues of fire.
Who has gobbled up the world's Justice?

Streams of blood, rivers of tears
The skies are bleached by terror.
The night is dark and numb
In the world of Hitler's power.

There are no more children playing or scampering.
Only massive graves of holy martyrs.
There are no more children to sing songs
In the country where my cradle once stood.

How can birds sing over that land?
How can flowers grow, nourished by the blood of children?
How can the sun shine with golden rays
when a million Jewish children have fallen?

יזכור

פון פרומע גולקאָװיטש-בערגער

עס איז יאָרצייט היינט — צעזייטאַגט איז מיין האַרץ,
און זע איך דעם טליען מיט'ן האַקיריקרייץ שװאַרץ.
װאָס האָט געמערדעט מיין פאָלק, — געברענט און געבראָטן,
דער װיכער דער בייזער — דעם אַ'ס האָט צעשאָטן.

יזכור איך זאָג נאָך אייך היילינע קדושים,
צעזייט און צעשפרייט אומצאַליגע מתים.
געהאָנגען איז אייער שׁולד — נאָר דאָס אייציגע זינד,
װאָס געטראָגן דעם נאָמען האָט איר, „אידיש קינד".

יזכור איך זאָג, יאָרצייט ליכם איך צינד,
פאַר מיליאָנען פאַרפייניגטע טאַטעס, מאַמעס און קינד.
פאַר ברידער געשעכטע, — איך פיל נאָך זייער װײ...
פאַר שװעסטער געשענדטע, —איך הער נאָך זייער געשריי !

יזכור איך זאָג, נאָך דיר אומבאַקאַנטער חעלה,
װאָס געפאַלן אין שלאַכט ביכמו אויף'ן בלוטיגן פעלה,
װי אַ שטאָלצער איד, װי אַ מוטינער פאַרטיזאַן,
באַװיזן דעם שׁונא, אז דער גײסט פון מכביער איז פאַראַן !

קדיש איך זאָג, נאָך אלע מיליאָנען,
עס ברענען די יאָרצייטסליכט — דער װעלט זיי דערמאָנען,
דעם אומגלייכן קאַמף פון רשעת מיט הילפלאָזער געטאָ.
װען געפאַלן האָט דער לעצטער, אין דער שׁעה שויך־שפעטער...

דער דור נאָך מיר פרעגט, צװייפלט און װאונדערט :
װי איז אַזאַ אכזריות געשען אין בהאַצ'גסטן יאָרהונדערט ?
איז דאָס די לאָגד פון גאָעטען, ניטשען און היינע
װאָס האָט אומגעבראַכט זעקס מיליאָן ברידער מיינע ?

אפשר איז דאָס אַלץ געװען אַ חלום אַ בייזער ?
נאָר איך אײנע װייס, אז נים געװען איז קיין דערלייזער !
װען עס האָבן קעפ געפאַלן, געשאָטן זיך אַריבער
קעפ בעשאָבעבע, קעפ פאַרבלוטיגטע — אין די טיפע שװאַרצע גריבער,

יזכור איך זאָג, — עס ברענט אין מיין מוח
און זע איך דעם חענקער, היטלער דעם רוצח,
מיין קאָפ איז געבויגן, מיין האַרץ איז פאַרקלעמט,
פרעג איך דער װעלט, — װי אזוי איז דיין פנים נים פאַרשעמט ?

YIZKOR

It is Yahrtzeit today – my heart is sorrowful.
As I see the glowing embers and the black Swastika
That murdered my people – burned and roasted.
The angry whirlwind has scattered their ashes.

I say Yizkor for you, holy martyrs,
Sown and scattered, uncountable corpses.
Your fault was – only that one sin –
You carried the name "Jewish child".

I say Yizkor, and I light Yahrtzeit candles
For the millions tormented – fathers, mothers, and children.
For slaughtered brothers – I still feel their pain.
For sisters, raped – I still hear their screams.

I say Yizkor for you, the unknown hero
Who fell in battle on the blood-soaked ground
As a proud Jew, a courageous Partisan,
You showed the enemy that the spirit
of the Maccabees still exists.

I say Kaddish for all the millions.
The Yahrtzeit candles burn to remind the world
Of the uneven battle of Evil against the helpless ghetto.
When the last one fell, the hour was already late.

The next generation asks, doubts, and wonders:
How could such brutality occur in the twentieth century?
Is this the land of Goethe, Nietzsche, and Heine
That annihilated six million of my brothers?

Maybe this was all a nightmare,
Only I alone know there was no savior!
When heads fell and were scattered all over
Heads shot, heads bloodied—in the deep, black pits.

I say Yizkor – it burns in my brain
And I see the executioner, Hitler, the murderer.
My head is bowed, my heart has tightened up -
And I ask the world:
"How can it be that your faces reflect no shame?"

זיעמליאַנקעס

פֿון פֿרומע גולקאָוויטש־בערגער

מײַן פֿרידלעך הײם פֿאַרניכט, בעטראַטן,
דער נאַצי וויל מײַן פֿאָלק אויסראָטן,
בין איך איצט דער וואַלד כאַוויער,
דער ביקס--נאַגאַן איז מײַן באַשיצער.

צווישן בוימער געדיכטע אין וואַלדיגן שטיל
שטיבלעך — זיעמליאַנקעס בויען מיר פֿיל,
מיט האַק און רידל איבערגעבויגן
פֿון טיפֿעניש אַרויס, קוקן נאָך וועלכישע אויגן.

פֿאַרמאַסקירט איז אין וועי ערד אַ טיפֿע גרוב
איז געוואָרן הײַנט מײַן שטוב,
אַן אַ נאַרע קײַן, האַרטער ברעט
איז געוואָרן הײַנט מײַן בעט.

צווײַגלעך פֿון יאָלקעס גרינעם
מאַכן גאָר מײַן געלעגער שווימען...
צוקאָפּנס דער ביקס, בײַם זײַט דער נאַגאַן,
און מען רופֿט מיר הײַנט, „פּאַרטיזאַן".

אַ פֿלעמל קוים טליעט בײַ דער נאַפֿט אין זײ
ווען עס זינגט אַ פּאַרטיזאַן פֿון „ווינד און ווײ"...
אין גרויען פֿרימאָרגן ווען איך וועק מיך אויף
געדיכטע איז די לופֿט, עס איבלט אין בויך.

אויף פֿלאַכיגן באָדן קײַן סימן נישטאָ
אַז אונטער דער ערד וואוינען אידן דאָ.
אין פֿראָסטיגן ווינטער באַדעקט זײ דער שנײ
מיט אַ ווײַסן טעפּיך באַפּוצט זײַנען זײ.

אַוועק די גרויע טעג, עס גרינט שיין אַרום
באַפוצט אין די זעמליאַנקעַ מיט גראָז און מיט בלום.
דאָס בלענדיגע ליכט פון זוניגן מאָרגן
איז שוין ניט מער פאַר אונז פאַרבאָרגן.

ווען עס צעשטורעמט זיך אין אַ זומער נאַכט,
רעגן און בליץ, און דונער עס קראַכט,
און וואָיעט זיך פאַנאַנדער דאָ דער ווינט
דאַכט זיך מיר — עס וויינט מיין שוועסטער'ס קינד..

דאָס וואַסער צווישן שטיינער זשומעט
שווער איז מיין פיין און טיף איז מיין אומעט,
גאָר הויבן אָן רוישן די בלעטער פון בוים
דאָן קומען חלומות פון האָפענונג און טרוים.

אין ליכט פון אויסגעטרוימטער שעה,
פון שוואַרץ די הימלען ווערן בלאָ,
גאָר אין מיין האַרץ ווי אַ ●כרי פון וואוגדן,
בריענט אַ „באָרן" — אָנגעצונדן !

ZIEMLANKAS

My peaceful home destroyed and trampled,
The Nazi seeks to eradicate my people
And I am now the forest's owner
The rifle and automatic pistol are my protection.

Between thick trees in the quiet of the forest
Little rooms – dugout bunkers – we are building many
With axe and spade, bent over.
Wolfish eyes stare out from the depths.

Hidden in the earth, a deep hole
Today became my home
And a hard wooden plank
my bed.

Twigs from green pine trees
Make my bed soft
The rifle is my headrest, by my side, the automatic pistol,
And now they call me "Partisan."

A tiny flame barely glows in the night
When a partisan sings of "wind and pain."
In the grey morning, when I awake
The air is putrid, nauseating.

On the flat roofs there are no signs
that there are Jews living underground.
In the frozen winter the snow covers them,
as if decorated with a beautiful white carpet.

Away the grey days, all around it is becoming green.
The dugout is covered with grass and with flowers,
The blinding light of the sunny morning
is no longer concealed from us.

When it is stormy on a summer night,
Rain and lightning, the crashing thunder
and the raging wind blow everything apart,
I imagine that my sister's child is crying.

The brook murmurs among stones.
Heavy is my pain and deep is my sorrow.
When the leaves in the trees begin to rustle,
Then dreams come of hope and visions of happiness.

In the light of the waking hour
From black, the skies become blue
But in my heart, like the sting of wounds
Burns a "Rage" only just ignited.

די שבועה

פֿון פֿרומע גולקאָװיטש־בערגער

עס איז געהאַטן אַמאָל אַ שטעטל,
קאָרעליטש האָט עס געהייסן.
אויסגעריסן איז דעם בלעטל,
פֿון פֿײן און צאָרן, נאָר מיר װײסן.
געיאָגט װי די הינם אונז פֿון אונזערע שטיבער,
אױף קידוש השם — צו די נאַװאַרעדקער גריבער,
געזען און געהערט אַלײן אַלע װײטן,
פֿון באַצעלע, פֿון מאַמעס, פֿון קינדער געשרײען —
'געשװאָרן האָב איך, אױף דעם קבר דעם גרויסן,
נים פֿאַרגעסן! נים פֿאַרגעבן! פֿאַר'ן בלום נאָך דעם הײסן.
און װאָס פֿאַר אַ נם איז מים מיר דאַן געשען?
איז דאָם דער זכות פֿון מײן פֿרומען טאַטן געװען?
די טײטלעבעע קול האָט אַם אין „ציל" נים געטראָפֿן.
איך שװוער אײך, ערד און הימל —
איר זאָלם עדות זײן אין דעם טאָג פֿון באַשטראַפֿן!
דער װינט האָט איצם דעם פֿלאַם צעטראָגן,
פֿון אַלע ברענענדיגע שטיבער
אַת איבער הויכע בערג, איבער גרינע טאָלן.
שרײַם מײַן חבר, דער פֿאַרטיזאַן, דער גיבור:
דײטשלאַנד! — פֿאַר אַלק, פֿאַר אַלק װעסטו נאָך באַצאָלן!
איך נעם דעם ביקס, איך גײן נאָך מײן חבר.
נקמה רופֿם! עם שרײַם פֿון קבר — בראַזוער.
שטעל דײַנע טרים! צו דעם װאָלד דעם געדיכטן,
פֿאַר די פֿאַרשניטענע לעבנם העלף דעם שונא פֿאַרניכטן!
דערלעבט פֿון שונא זען נקמה,
אַבער עלענד און טרױער איז אױף מײן נשמה,
װײל נאָך אײך, מײנע טײערסטע בענק איך אַזױ שטאַרק,
אײך צו פֿאַרגעבן איז נישטאָ אױ מעכט!

THE PLEDGE

There once was a little town,
It was called Korelitz.
The page has been torn out
by pain and fury.
But we know.
Routed like dogs from our homes,
As blessed martyrs – to the pits of Novogrudek.

I saw and heard everyone crying,
Fathers and mothers, children screaming,
I swore, on the big mass grave
Not to forget! Not to forgive! For the blood that was still hot.
And what a miracle then happened to me!
Was it in the merit of my pious father?
The lethal bullet missed its "target."
I swear to you, heaven and earth:
You shall bear witness on the day of reckoning.

The wind has now spread the flames
From all the burning houses
And over high hills, over green valleys.
My friend, the partisan, the hero shouts:
"Germany! For everything – everything, you will yet pay!"
I take the rifle and follow my friend
Revenge is calling! It is calling from the graves:
"Courageous ones!
Make your way to the thick forest.
For the cut-down lives, help destroy the enemy!"
I lived to see revenge on the enemy ~
But alone, and grief burdens my soul.
Because, my loved ones, I miss you so dearly.
There is no power that could make me forget you!

די צוואה

פֿון פֿרומע גולקאָוויטש - בערגער

ווען איך בין נאָך קליין געווען,
האָב איך די וועלט גאָר אין שיינע פֿאַרבן געזען,
בלימעלאָך פֿון צויבער קאַלירן, באַדעקן די ערד־מאַמען,
אין די געלאַדענע זונשטראַלן באַשיינען די פֿאַנאַראַמע.

ווי איך האָב נאָר אונטערגעוואַקסן גרעסער
האָב איך שוין פֿיל זאַכן באַנומען בעסער,
אַז אין די וועלדער לעבן חיות וואָס טויטן,
אַז די ערד־מאַמע ווערט אָפֿט באַגאָסן מיט בלוט רויטן.

אַז אַ וואָלף עסט אויף אַ שעפֿס, אַ בֿאַראַן,
אַז אויך מענטשן זיינען אַזעלכע פֿאַראַן,
בלוט־דורשטיגע חיות, אין מענטשן געשטאַלט,
וואָס עס פֿאַרניכטן שוואַכערע, האַרצלאָזיג, קאַלט.

ווען איך בין שוין גרויס געוואָרן,
האָב איך פֿאַרשאַלטן דעם טאָג פֿון געבאָרן,
ווייל היטלער ימח שמו האָט די מאַכט פֿאַרכאַפּט,
די אידן אין די קאָנצענטראַציע־לאַגערן פֿאַרפּאַקט.

געפּייניגט, געהונגערט, ארויסגעוויגט דאָס לעצטע ביסל בלום,
פֿון אַלם, פֿון יונג, — דאָס קינד איז גֿלייך געווען ניט גוט,
אין די נאַזיקאַמערן דערשטיקט, געוואָרפֿן אין די פֿייערבוזעגן,
אומגעבראַכט מיין פֿאָלק, מיליאָנען פֿאַרשלונגען.

היינט, ווען האָב דעם קאָשמאַר דורכגעלעבט,
ניט איינמאָל פֿאַר די אויגן האָב דער טויט געשוועבט,
האָב איך געזען אַז די וועלט האָט אויך פֿאַרבן שוואַרצע גרויע,
ווייל איך פֿאַר מיינע קינדער לאָזן אַ צוואה.

קיינמאָל ניט פֿאַרגעסן די מאַרטירער פֿון די זעקס מיליאָן
זיין שטאַלץ צו בראַגן די ווייסביליווע פֿאָן,
קעמפֿן פֿאַר אַ וועלט האו אַלע מענטשן זיינען פֿריי,
בויען אין דאָס אייגן לאַנד, אַ לעבן אַ ניי !

THE WILL

When I was still small,
I saw the world only in beautiful colors.
Flowers of enchanting hues covered Mother Earth
And the golden rays of the sun shone upon the vista.

As I grew a bit older,
I understood many things better:
That in the forests there are beasts that kill;
That Mother Earth is often drenched with red blood.

Just as a wolf devours a sheep or a goat,
So too there exist people,
Blood-thirsty animals in human form,
Who heartlessly and coldly destroy the weak.

When I was finally grown up
I cursed the day that I was born
Because Hitler, may his name be obliterated, seized power
And packed the Jews into concentration camps.

Tortured, starved, sucked out the last drop of blood
From old, from young –
even a child was thought already worthless.
Suffocated in the gas chambers,
thrown into the tongues of flame,
My people killed, millions swallowed up.

Today, having lived through the nightmare,
Death having floated before my eyes more than once,
I have seen that the world
also has colors in shades of grey.
I want to leave my children a will:

Never forget the martyrdom of the six million.
Be proud to carry the white-blue flag.
Fight for a world where all people are free.
Build – in your own land – a new life!

די געטא

פון פרומע גולקאוויטש-בערגער

היטלער-נאצי האט פארכאפט אונזערע, געביטן
אין גליך געכאפט הערטן מיט גרויזאמע זיטן
געכטים פאר אידן געטאס מיט הויכע װענם
געפינזגט, געמאָרדעטן, אין אזיהנם געברענם.

א הויכע װאנם, מיט שטעכיגע דראטן
זיי פון א תפיסה איז ארויסגיין פארבאטן
א װאך פון אויבן, א װאך פון ארום
אוז די װאם אינמיטן — זיינען צום אומקום.

געטריבן האט דער נאצי היטנער געטאיװאנם אלע
אלמע, יונגע, אייך פארליבטע חתן-כלה.
שרעקלעך זיינען די לייין היטנער'ן װאנם
אן רחמנות די הערשער פון היטלעריאנער.

װאם איז די ארבעט, װאם איז דער שיין?
מעז האט אונז פארפירט אין „חדר" אריין,
אידן שטארבן פון הונגער, פון פיין און שמוץ
אלע טאג טויטע — ביי דעם מוק.

געפאנגען האט דער פלאם פון שנאה בלינדער
אלע שרעלעך אומברארבט: באטעם, מאטעם, פיצלעך קינדער
אונטער ביקסן צום מאסקרבר געטריבן זיי זיך אויסטאָן
די ערד איז שנעל אנטרונגען פון אונטער די אנטבלויזטע.

אין די װעלט געװעזן איז בליזה, געװעזן איז טויב,
גיט געװעז װי מענטש פארזאנדלם מענטש אין אש און שטויב
גיט געהערט פון קינדער די געװיינען די געשרייען
פון אלטע לייט די זיפצן און די שטילע װיינען...

פון די אידן אין געטא גיט געבליבן איז קיין שפור
פון די קרבנות די זאבן — א פור נאך א פור,
דער נאצי-מערדער האט מים ביקס און פלאם
פארטיליגט ביז'ן װארצל אונזער דורות'דיגן שטאם

פאראוווסט די היימען, פוסט זיינען די הייזער אונטער דעכער
פארבליבן נאר פון טוים א צינד די שװארצע לעכער
און איבער זיי די היטלען אן רחמנות פוסט און לער
אלץ װאם קענען העלפן איז צו געבן נאך א טרער...

THE GHETTO

Hitler-Nazis seized our neighborhoods,
And immediately started to rule with brutal edicts,
Built ghettos with high walls for Jews,
Tortured, murdered, burnt in the ovens.

A high wall, with barbed wire.
Like a prison, it was forbidden to leave.
Guards above, guards all around —
And those in the middle – are to be destroyed.

The Nazis drove everyone between the ghetto-walls:
Old, young, brides and grooms in love.
The suffering is horrible behind the wall
The rulers of Hitler-land have no compassion.

What kind of work? What kind of certificate?
They misled us into "school."
Jews are dying of hunger, from pain and filth.
Everyday there are corpses – by the dozen.

The flames of blind hatred took prisoners.
All were murdered in an appalling manner:
fathers, mothers, tiny children.
They were forced, under rifles,
to the mass graves to undress.
The ground quickly disappeared under the naked corpses.

And the world was blind and deaf,
It did not see how man turned his fellow man
to ash and dust.
It did not hear the children crying and screaming
Or the sighing and the quiet moaning of the elderly...

No vestige remained of the Jews in the ghetto
Not of the victims nor wagonload
after wagonload of their belongings.
The Nazi murderer, with gun and flame,
Eradicated the stock of our generations to the very root.

Our homes are desolate – empty under their roofs.
Now, only the black holes of death remain
And over them the skies without pity, empty and void.
All that can help is to shed another tear...

THE LITTLE ORPHAN

Tell me little girl, pray say,
Why your sorrow, fears?
Your large, black and lovely eyes
Why always full of tears?

"I bear a sorrow, aye I bear,
I to no one in the world can call,
Father, mother have been killed
When I was still quite small.

Grandma, grandpa, too, are slain
In the woods where the large trench turned,
Brothers, sisters of my faith
In one room they all were burned.

Our goods and all for which we toiled
From all our Jewish people there,
The Nazis took away from us
And sent us forth to death, despair.

Like an abandoned stone I'm left,
And I am quite alone,
I have remained quite desolate
Sans family or home.

Sorrow I bear and fear
That in the world alone am I,
My dear ones murdered, doomed to die,
When I was still so small."

דער העלד-אפרים

פון פרומע גולקאָוויטש-בערגער

פאַרוואָס ? פאַרוואָס ? אויב עס איז אַ זין אין מײַן פאַראָן,
וועל איך נקמה נעמען פאַר אײַך, שוועסטער אפרים דער פּאַרטיזאַן.
נעכטן ערשט געשמאַכט אין געטאָ, מיט אַ געבויגן פּלײיצע,
געזען, גיטאָ קיין נסים הײַנט, געזוכט האָט ער אַ עצה.

אַ שטים אַ שטילע האָט ער געטרופן, אין דער שוואַרצער נאַכט,
עס קומט פון גרויסן מאַסן־קבר, פון דעם טיפסטן שאַכט.
איך זען דעם ליכטיגן געשטאַלט און הער דעם פּליסטער פון מײַן כלה,
געדענק : נקמה מוזשׁוּ נעמען פאַר אונז אַלע !

אָט זע איך איצט דעם לעצטן בליק פון זייער לעצטער שעה,
דער שווידער פון דעם לעצטן ווי פון מאַמעם, מאַטעם דאָ
און אַזוי פיל קלײנע הענטלעך עס רופן מיך אַצינד,
נקמה זאָלסטו נעמען, פאַר יעדן אומגעבראַכטן קינד !

איך וועל די מערדער ניט פאַרגעבן,
נקמה פאַר אײַך איז מײַן ציל אין לעבן,
מאַנען וועל איך בלוט פאַר בלוט,
צו פאַרניכטן דעם שונא וועל איך קעמפן מיט מוט !

פאַראויס, פאַראויס, ער לויפט אויף זײַן ווײַסן פערד,
ווי אַ האָן אַ פליִנקער, ער רירט גים אָן די ערד.
דער אַטאַמאַט אויף זײַן אַקסל, מיט'ן נאַגאַן אין האַנט,
טראַגט ער פײַער צום שונא, וואָ נאַר ער שפּאַנט.

ווי אַ פלאַמיגער פויגל, ווי אַן אָדלער, ער פלים,
מיט שטאָלץ וויל ער טראָגן דעם נאַמען „איד".
דער ערשטער אין קאַמף, ווי אַ טיגער, אַ חיה —
מאַכט ער דעם שונא חורבונות נײַע.

אָבער געפאַלן אין שלאַכט איז דער פּאַרטיזאַן אפרים —
באַווײַנט האָבן דעם העלד, אפילו די גויים.
דאָרט אונטער דעם בערגל, בײַ דער הױכער בוים,
ליגט אַ שטאָלצער איד — צוואַנציג יאָר קוים.

געלאָזן פאַר דער וועלט וועלט האָט ער אַן אָנזאָג, אַ פּאַראָל,
צו טראָגן דעם גײַסט פון די חשמונאים, פון אַמאָל.
נקמה צו נעמען פאַר אַלע וואָס זײַנען פריציייטיג
געוואָרן דורך דעם העלקער פון דער וועלט באַזײַיטיגט.

געווידמעט מײַן קוזין, אפרים גולקאָוויטש, וועלכער איז געפאַלן
אין קאַמף (מײַ, 1944), אין טשקאַלאָווסקער בריגאַדע

THE HERO – EPHRAIM

"Why? Why? If there is any sense in death,
I will take revenge for you," swears Ephraim, the Partisan.
Yesterday, still suffering in the ghetto, with a bowed back,
Having seen that there were no miracles today
He searched for an idea.

A quiet voice called in the black night
It came from the big mass grave, from the deepest pit.
"I see the vision of light and hear the whisper from my bride,
'Remember, you must take revenge for all of us.'"

"Now I see their final look, from their last hour,
The shudders of the final agony of mothers and fathers.
And so many little hands are calling me now.
'You must take revenge for every slaughtered child.'"

"I will not forgive the murderers.
Revenge for you is my purpose in life,
I will demand blood for blood.
To destroy the enemy, I will fight with courage."

Forward, forward he races on his white horse,
Nimble as a hare, he does not touch the ground.
The automatic rifle on his shoulder,
the automatic pistol in his hand
He carries fire to the enemy, wherever he goes.

Like a flaming bird, as an eagle he flies,
With pride he wants to carry the name "Jew."
The first in the fight, as a tiger, a beast,
He brings the enemy new destruction.

But he fell in the battle,
The Partisan Ephraim,
Even the gentiles mourned for him.
There by the mound, near the tall tree,
Lies a proud "Jew," hardly twenty years old.

He left the world a testament, a pledge,
To carry the spirit of the Hasmoneans of long ago,
To take revenge for all those who were so early destroyed
by the murderers, and taken away from the world.[x]

Tears and Poems of a Jewish Woman

Translated and excerpted from the original Yiddish
"Tears And Poems Of A Jewish Woman"
By Y. Shmulevitsch, *Jewish Daily Forward*, January 27, 1968

In front of me sat an attractive woman. Her large eyes were full of loneliness and sorrow. She was silent and looked straight ahead. It was immediately apparent that she constantly thinks about something that steadily accompanies her present life.

"I'm not a literary artist," Fruma Gulkowich Berger said, "but I write poems. These poems heal my wounds after the terrible things I lived through under Hitler. They are also a sort of eternal monument for my dear and near ones, for the Jews of my former home town, for all those whose lives were cut short by the Hitler murderers."

Fruma placed a small bundle of poems on my writing table. The names of the poems, written in large, black letters, looked up at me: "Bread in the Ghetto." "Memorial Candles." "Efraim, the Hero." "Yizkor." It seemed as though the dead letters on the sheets of paper suddenly acquired a living tongue. It seemed as though the room we were sitting in was suddenly filled with noises. Souls fluttered around us, the souls of murdered Jewish men and women, children and old folks. They came to hear what Fruma would tell me.

It happened in the Jewish town of Korelitz, between Novaredok (Novogrudek) and Mir, in the region of Baranovitsh, Russia where about 1,500 Jews lived. They were warm and caring Jews who enjoyed a long and honorable ancestry. Among them were Fruma Gulkowich and her family.

When the Second World War broke out in September 1939, Korelitz was occupied by the Soviet forces. Jewish life was suddenly and completely transformed. It wasn't the same as before. But the Jews adjusted to the new circumstances and they kept on with confidence and hope.

All of a sudden this new life was disrupted as well. On June 22, 1941 Hitler unexpectedly attacked Soviet Russia. The lives of the Jews in Korelitz, as elsewhere, were transformed into a living hell.

"Right at the beginning," Fruma relates, "we were driven into a ghetto in Korelitz. I was there with my mother, my father, three sisters and brother. It was very difficult. There was no limit to our suffering and pain. In December 1941, local Nazi collaborators, headed by a man named Briczkowsky, beat my mother until she died of her wounds. I will never forget that."

Suddenly one day in 1942, all the Jews were herded together in the marketplace in Korelitz. Fruma and her three sisters, Grunia, Feigele and Brina, were among them. Their father Shloyme stood next to the girls. He could barely stand on his swollen feet.

The Nazis and their local helpers forced the Jews to start marching. The "march" was accompanied by blows and curses as the guards encircled the Jews, their rifles cocked. "That day felt like an eternity for the Jews," tells Fruma.

"Finally, in the evening," she continues, "we arrived at

Novogrudek. We were exhausted and in pain, hungry and thirsty. We were driven like dogs into stalls in the Peresica Ghetto. The Jews of Novogrudek, as well as the surrounding towns, including Lubtsh, Ivenitse, Nalibok, Wseilub and others, were there as well. An endless chain of sorrow and pain began for all of us."

Fruma's eyes grew even sadder. She sighs deeply and begins to relate how the local Jews were killed. She also relates the remarkable account of her rescue.

It was Friday morning, August 7, 1942. Suddenly the ghetto was surrounded by the Nazis and their collaborators. All the Jews in the Peresica Ghetto were herded together into one place. They had to lie on the ground with their faces down. Then they were all herded to Litovke, on the road between Novogrudek and Wseilub. Huge pits had been prepared there. All the Jews—men and women—had to strip naked. Immediately afterward all the Jews were shot and their bodies were thrown into open pits.

Earlier, the Jewish children had been asphyxiated in special "death-trucks" and they too were buried in the mass graves. The horrible slaughter of the Jews was carried out, under the supervision of German Nazis, by Lithuanians, Ukrainians, Estonians, Latvians and White Russians.

When the Nazis were preparing for the slaughter, they told the leaders of the *Judenrat* and the Jewish police that if they helped carry out the *aktion*, their lives would be spared. But after the Jews had been driven onto the field of slaughter, most of the leaders of the *Judenrat* and the Jewish ghetto police were brought there as well and they were shot along with the others.

"When the Jews were driven from the ghetto," Fruma tells, "I quickly ran into the barn where my family had stayed. I met my father there. He stood in a corner wrapped in his *tallis*, reading Psalms incessantly. My father didn't say a word. All he did was continue reading Psalms, and he looked at me with petrified eyes. He too, this pious Jew, was taken by the murderers to the pits, where a bullet killed him. I can't forget how he looked at me…"

I asked Fruma:"How did you survive that terrible slaughter?"

"I don't know," she said, "whether you've ever heard anything like this. It's altogether incredible. I'll tell you…"

*　　*　　*　　*

"In the great panic, when death lurked on all sides, my sister-in-law Yehudis tugged at my arm. "Come on, let's find a place to hide," she said. But where could we find a hole to crawl into? The earth wasn't willing to open up and conceal us.

"We hurried along. On the way we saw murdered Jews. I recognized one of the victims. It was Marke Yelin from Korelitz. She had spat in a Nazi's face and he shot her.

"Yehudis and I were passing by the communal outhouse that was in the middle of the ghetto. Without thinking a minute we went in—and that was where we hid. We climbed into the pit of filthy excrement that covered us up to our necks. Two other women were already there: Esther Menaker and Mashe Rabinovitsh. Each of us moved toward one of the four corners of the pit, so that if anyone heard one of us breathing, the rest wouldn't be discovered."

Fruma further relates that while she lay in the filth, she constantly heard Nazis running to and fro in the ghetto, looking for concealed Jews. The four women heard the Nazis driving the Jews to the ghetto at Litevske. They heard shots, along with the weeping of children and the barking of dogs."

"Suddenly," exclaims Fruma, "a Nazi entered the outhouse in order to relieve himself, and the excrement fell on our heads. At that moment we held our breaths and sunk ourselves so deep that the filth almost covered us. I tasted the excrement in my mouth.

"The Nazis had brought dogs and the dogs started barking.

It was clear to them that Jews must be hiding somewhere here. So they began shooting into the cesspool."

One bullet struck Esther, who fell dead into the filth. A second bullet struck Fruma, but only slightly wounded her in the right arm. Finally the Nazis and the dogs left. The women heard them remark that, if anyone were still alive in the filth, they would probably die sooner or later anyway.

Fruma, Yehudis and Mashe hid in the pit of excrement for a full six days without eating or drinking. "Worms ate our bodies," Fruma said, "and itched us terribly. Our clothes had rotted away. Every time someone came into the outhouse to relieve himself, our hearts stopped from terror. We were ready to surrender to the Nazis because it was impossible to hold on. Perhaps we didn't have the strength to climb out of the pit..."

On the seventh day, Fruma's brother Ben-Zion Gulkowich arrived in the ghetto. He was part of a group of Jews who had been sent to work cleaning up the ghetto. Somehow he learned of the women's hiding place and risked his life to pull his sister Fruma, his wife Yehudis, and Mashe from the filth, saving the three women from certain death.

*   *   *   *

Eventually they all took a risk and escaped from the ghetto. A group of twenty-five Jewish men and women who had stayed hidden and thus managed to escape the slaughter at Litovke, made their way into the nearby woods and joined the partisan fighters.

Fruma was the first woman to receive a rifle. Ben-Zion was one of the heroic partisans and excelled as a scout. Fruma's three sisters, just like her mother and father, died at the hands of the Nazis.

While in the forest, Fruma became acquainted with Motkeh Berger, who was from Wseilub. He was a member of the first group of Jewish partisans who left the Novaredok ghetto for the

Naliboki forests, where they helped to organize the famous Bielski Brigade.

Until July 1944, when the Red Army came and liberated them, they all were in the Naliboki forests. Soon after the liberation Fruma and Motkeh returned to Novaredok and remained there until the end of 1944, when they went to Lublin, Poland.

They left Poland in 1945, thanks to the underground *aliyah*, and made their way to Italy, where they were married.

There the couple lived in "Kibbutz Anzio," a special DP camp for former partisans. They were to have traveled to Israel, but the way was blocked by the British. At that time, Motkeh Berger located his oldest brother Herzl, living in Massachusetts, who had been in America since 1912.

The Bergers arrived in America in 1947 and eventually had two sons, Albert and Ralph. Ben-Zion and his wife Yehudis also made it to America, as did Motke's brother Elye.

"In my former home town of Korelitz," Fruma said to me at the end of the interview, "I belonged to a drama group. I was active in Yiddish cultural events. I wrote poems and other pieces and presented readings of them on various occasions. After the Holocaust at the hands of the Nazis, I set myself to the task of writing down my experiences, mostly in verse. Here's some of it.

Read…"

The first candle I light in memory of you, my mother,
Who is remained in your lonesome grave?
Dark and searing was the pain
when your soul departed your body.
In black clouds arise figures
of the dreadful injustice which the world concealed.
So much sorrow in every shadow;
the blood still flows and silently demands to be staunched.

Or:

Yizkor I say; it burns in my brain.
And I see the swastika, Hitler the murderer;
My head is bowed, my heart is weighed down.
And I ask the world;
"How can your face reflect no shame?"

A Jew from the Forests

Translated and excerpted from the original Yiddish
"A Jew From The Forests"
By Y. Shmulevitsch, *Jewish Daily Forward*, September 7, 1968

On the other side of the ocean, where the many-branched oak called Eastern European Jewry was once to be found, there were countless deeply-rooted Jewish towns that traced their ancestry back for many generations. Most of those communities were completely obliterated. No trace of them remains after the dreadful Nazi flood poured through that part of the world. One of those towns was Wseilub, in the area of Novogrudek, which was in the White Russian portion of inter-war Poland.

Only a few people from that *shtetl* survived—so few that they can be counted on the fingers of both hands. Some of them are now living in America and the rest in the State of Israel. Even those few who had miraculously survived were on the verge of dying at the hands of the Nazis. But they decided to risk their lives in an attempt to escape, and thus they avoided transformation into cinders and skeletons.

They set off for the forests, and there, together with other Jews, they became partisans, fighting against Hitler's soldiers.

One of the forest Jews and few survivors from Wseilub was Motkeh Berger. Berger's wife Fruma (nee Gulkowich) also lived through the Nazi hell.

"Our town of Wseilub," related Berger, "was small. Only about a hundred Jewish families lived there. But the town was rich in Judaism, with a deeply and broadly ramified Jewish life."

Wseilub boasted a range of Jewish groups and societies. Everything was soaked in Jewishness. Young people from the town travelled to study in *yeshivas* and eventually grew into great rabbis.

Jewish youth from Wseilub also set out for the great cities of Poland in the years before the war. There they were active and eventually became responsible, experienced members of various Jewish nationalist, secular, cultural, social and other organizations. Others set off for Eretz Israel. They were Zionist pioneers and were among the builders and shapers of the Jewish state.

"Our heritage, the heritage of Wseilub Jews," says Berger, "is a great one. As far back as 64 years ago, in 1904, new arrivals from Wseilub in New York organized a mutual aid society, which is still accomplishing important work. The people from Wseilub here are active in various social and philanthropic efforts. That is how it has been from year to year.

All of us survivors from Wseilub, wherever we may find ourselves, guard the heritage of our small and precious hometown."

But Berger finds no rest. Why, he asks, is the obliteration of the town and its Jews nowhere related? "It's an outrage!"

Berger 's grandfather, "Leybe, the Mountain Man," lived on a high mountain in Wseilub (this is the source of the family name). His grandfather owned fields, stores and other possessions. He was known throughout the region as a prominent merchant. Motkeh's father Avrom-Tsvi and his wife Sora were involved in commerce as well.

His two sisters and two of his brothers, along with their spouses and children, were killed by the Nazis. Another brother, Herzl, arrived in America more than fifty years ago and has since died. His surviving brother Elye and his wife Rena live in New York.

"When the Second World War broke out," Berger relates, "our town of Wseilub, like the entire surrounding region, was occupied by the Soviets. We hoped the times would get better. But suddenly the dreadful catastrophe came. At the end of June 1941, immediately after Hitler attacked the Soviet Union, the German Nazi hordes came to our town. A time of troubles, suffering and pain began for us."

Berger says that it is impossible to describe the terrible suffering the Jews withstood at the hands of the Nazis and their local collaborators. The Jews were forced to do hard labor; they were tormented and beaten. Jews were taken out to the fields and shot there. "Jewish blood flowed like water," he said.

That was the period when Berger escaped from Wseilub. He set off for the nearby town of Novogrudek.

"From that day on," he relates, "I no longer saw my town or my family. Through fields and forests, tired and depressed, I barely made my way to Novogrudek. There I faced new troubles and torments, together with the local Jews."

Right at the start, the Nazis shot 120 Jews in Novogrudek. Among them were the leading householders of the city and the members of the *intelligentsia*. Such *aktions* took place repeatedly until December 1941, when a ghetto was established in Novogrudek and new slaughters began shortly afterward.

"On Friday, December 5, 1941," Berger relates, "we received the news that outside of the city, near the village of Skridleve, large pits were being dug. People also said that the city of Novogrudek had already been surrounded on all sides so that no one could escape. All of this made it clear that there would be a huge massacre, as had already happened in other towns and cities nearby.

"I decided that I wasn't going to wait around to walk into the pits alive. If death had to come, let the bullet come from behind. And maybe fate would see to it that the bullet missed."

When night fell, Berger escaped. He made his way out of the Novogrudek ghetto and set off. Shortly thereafter, the Nazis and their collaborators did indeed carry out a horrible massacre against the Jews of Novogrudek. Jews from Wseilub were among those killed. The massacre took place on Monday, December 8, 1941.

"Christians later reported," said Berger, "that the wailing and shrieking of the desperate Jews reached to the heavens. But no help came. The day after the massacre, when four thousand Jews from Novogrudek and the surrounding area were shot and buried alive, the earth still trembled and collapsed in places from the streams of blood that ran off for quite a distance."

Berger wandered here and there, with cold and hunger as his companions, like a hunted animal. He looked death in the eyes many times. There were some places where he was hidden by Christians, but he was always in danger.

His situation was so dreadful that after several months, he decided on his own to return to the Novogrudek ghetto, where a few Jews still remained. "It was like walking into the lion's maw," he said

Even this wasn't easy to accomplish. With great effort, he barely managed to make his way back into the ghetto. There were newly arrived Jews there, people from the towns of Lubtsh, Korelitz, Ivenets, Golibok, Nayshtot, Rebzevitsh, Steypts and others.

The conditions in the ghetto were awful and everyone was panicked because there were rumors that the Nazis were preparing for another massacre.

"I decided then," Berger continues, "that I would leave the ghetto as soon as possible, before it became too late. Several young people approached me because they knew that I was very well acquainted with the surrounding area. Our idea was to get in touch with the partisans and join them in fighting the Nazis and thus take our revenge. We then got word that the Bielski brothers wanted to form a unit. As soon as we had worked out our plan, we escaped from the ghetto. We took a chance and it worked. We went to the forest to join the partisans."

Those who escaped from the ghetto with Berger at the beginning of August 1942 included Yisroel Yankelevitsh, Aron Lubtshansky, Pesakh Fridberg, Yudel Levin and Yudel Bell. They all came to live in America.

Shortly afterward, on August 7, 1942, the Nazis and their local helpers murdered nearly all the Jews who remained in Novogrudek and the surrounding area. A total of 4,000 Jews including men, women, young people and small children were shot by the murderers.

"The Nazi regional commissar in Novogreudek, a man named Traub who was a famous anti-Semite," says Berger, "received a personal commendation from Hitler for his persecution and murder of the Jews."

Berger, together with the other Jews who had miraculously escaped certain death, arrived at the forest where a Jewish partisan unit was being established. A company was organized—the Bielski Brigade—with Tuvia Bielski as commander. Those heroic partisans, the forest Jews, including Motkeh Berger, carried out an important struggle against the Nazis. They made a significant contribution to Hitler's defeat. They fought in the endless Naliboki forests, in the Lubetshansk wilderness and in other areas.

Those heroic, fearless Jews wrote a wonderful chapter in the scroll of Jewish resistance and heroism in the time of the Second World War.

"When they gave me a rifle in the forest," Berger continues, "I wished that the rifle would help me to take revenge in the name of my family and for all the Jews, and that I would be able to return to the city with the rifle. My wish came true.

"In the spring of 1944, when Hitler was defeated and we left the forest, I went to Novogrudek and Wseilub with the rifle that had served me during my years as a partisan. But there were no Jews there—no sign of a Jewish life!"

"And that is how it was in the entire region," Berger concluded, "Everything had disappeared, completely wiped out."

Afterword: In the Words of Their Children – Ralph and Albert Berger

Our parents did not think of themselves as heroes. Others did, however, including us as we got older and more fully appreciated all they had gone through and achieved. Neither of us will ever forget a bat mitzvah we attended a few years ago in California. A well-dressed, stately looking lady began to run towards us, limping and shouting "You're Murray Berger's sons. You're Murray Berger's sons." A middle-aged man followed behind. He was smiling and trying to keep up with his mother. When she reached us and caught her breath, she explained, "I'm Tamara Katz. Your father carried me and my son out of the ghetto." Until then, we had never heard this story.

At a young age, we knew about World War II and the Holocaust and the destruction of our extended family. But we knew little about our parents' lives between then and our early childhood years. The fact that they had survived the War and were among the Jews who had fought back in order to do so was what was important; the struggles that followed were merely obstacles they had to overcome.

Life was not easy for our parents after the War. They were truly "displaced persons" in every sense of the word. They had lost, under horrific circumstances, most of their families, their friends, their possessions and their way of life. There was no way of going back. The world that they had known no longer existed.

After the liberation, our parents and our Uncle Ben and Aunt Judy went back to their old homes in Poland. There was still fighting going on and it was obvious that the Poles did not want any of their former Jewish neighbors coming back and trying to reclaim whatever possessions were left that were rightfully theirs.

Their homes had been taken over by Poles from the area and these people were shocked to see our parents and Ben and Judy. They had presumed them dead along with all the Jews from Korelitz who had been slaughtered. They acted as if they were seeing ghosts and then denied that our parents and aunt and uncle had ever lived there. Our parents and aunt and uncle had to fight their way back into Ben and Judy's former home, if only for a little while.

Uncle Ben and Aunt Judy had been married before the war, and before they were forced into the Novogrudek ghetto, they had buried gold that had belonged to Judy's family inside their house. Once they got back into their house, they unearthed the gold and then fled. The gold helped the four of them go from country to country across Europe, looking for a place of refuge.

At each border crossing, there were patrols that confiscated everything of value the survivors had, claiming that it would be later returned. Our parents and Ben and Judy were searched constantly. Women were forced to jump up and down in order to dislodge any valuables that might be hidden in a body cavity.

At one border crossing, Aunt Judy bit her gums to make them bleed and disguised the gold as an ice pack for her "toothache." Only then was she allowed to cross the border without being searched, with the gold literally in hand. When they finally reached Rome, Uncle Ben had signet rings made from some of the gold for himself, Judy, our parents and our Uncle Ellie, Dad's brother. Mom's and Dad's rings are in our possession to this day and we always wear them on High Holidays.

As they traveled east, they told authorities they were returning home. In this manner they went from Belarus to Poland and from there to Romania, where Mom worked as a cook in a DP (Displaced Persons) camp. After leaving Romania, they went to Yugoslavia and finally wound up in Italy. Many people along the way were former partisans willing to help fellow partisans. The Serbs were especially friendly to partisans, as they had waged a similar war themselves against the Nazis.

When the group got to Rome, they stayed for two years until they decided what to do next. Mom and Dad worked at different jobs, as did Uncle Ben, Aunt Judy and Uncle Ellie. It was in Rome that Mom and Dad married.

While on a trip to Rome several years ago, Ralph was able to find the listing of our parents' marriage in a ledger in the archive of the old Rome synagogue on the Tiber River. The entry for February 14, 1947 had our parents' signatures, our mother's maiden name, the places where both our parents were from, the signatures of two witnesses and the signature of the presiding rabbi.

In the DP camp in Rome, our parents met an American army reporter who spoke Yiddish. Dad told him that his oldest brother Harry had left Wseilub and immigrated to America as a teenager and had served as a soldier in the U.S. army during World War I. From letters that Uncle Harry had written, Dad recalled that Harry lived in an American town whose name translated into "jumping fields." The reporter helped them figure out that the town was "Springfield." However, which of the many Springfields in the United States it was remained a mystery.

Notices were placed in Jewish War Veterans newspapers in each state that had a town called Springfield. It turned out that Uncle Harry was living in Springfield, Massachusetts. He was married to Ruth, an American schoolteacher. It so happened that Aunt Ruth had read the notice in the newspaper and then excitedly told Uncle Harry that two of his brothers, Dad and Uncle Ellie, had survived the war.

Since Dad's brother Harry was in the United States, our parents preferred to come to the U.S. rather than go to Israel or South Africa, where Mom had three aunts, all of whom had emigrated before the war, married and raised large families. In fact, Mom had been slated to immigrate to South Africa in 1939, but by the time she had all of the necessary papers, it was too late. The Nazis would not allow Jews to leave Poland.

One of our South African cousins, Sam Pogorelsky, told us about the tremendous excitement in his parents' home in Johannesburg when they received a letter from Mom in Rome, telling them that she, Ben and Judy had survived. When Sam's father Gerson heard about our parents' survival, he told his landlord about it and his landlord enlisted the help of his son, a pilot in the South African Air Force, who flew to Rome quite often. In this way, Sam's parents sent stockings and foodstuffs and other necessary items to Rome to make our parents' lives a little easier.

While in Rome, Mom taught herself English and was able to write to her cousins (the Hills and the Orloffs) in Chicago. They subsequently agreed to "sponsor" (guarantee that one would not become a ward of the state) Ben and Judy and their son who had been born in Italy, our cousin Albert. Uncle Harry sponsored Mom, Dad and Uncle Ellie. Dad's uncle, Sam Shmulevicz of Brooklyn, NY, paid the fees associated with their passage to America and is also listed as a sponsor on the transport papers.

Once passage was arranged they set sail on the ship *Marine Flasher* from Marseilles, France to the United States. Our parents and Uncle Ellie arrived in New York harbor on April 15, 1947. Uncle Ben, Aunt Judy and our cousin Al soon followed.

After they arrived in the U.S., our parents went from Springfield to Chicago and settled in New York. For several years, our parents and Uncle Ellie lived on the Lower East Side of Manhattan in a tenement apartment with a shared bathroom on Eldridge Street. Dad and Uncle Ellie went to the Turkish baths to bathe and Mom used the kitchen sink as her bathtub. Al was born in November 1947.

Dad struggled to make a living. He tried being a butcher and selling paper bags to stores. Since he had powerful arms and shoulders, he was able to find work on construction sites that had sprung up because of the surge in home building after WWII. Dad worked construction during the day and went to school at night to learn English. He did well and was able to save up enough money to buy a house in a middle class section in the Bronx, where Uncle Ellie also lived until he married Aunt Rena, who was a concentration camp survivor. Ralph was born in August 1952, on the tenth anniversary of the massacre in the Novogrudek ghetto in which many of our relatives were killed.

However, by the mid 1950s, prosperity was declining and Dad wasn't getting as much construction work. Additionally, he was over forty years old and manual labor was getting difficult. After being out of work for a while, our parents couldn't afford to keep the Bronx house and were forced to sell it.

Uncle Ellie was working as a typesetter at a Yiddish newspaper, the legendary *Forward*. He helped Dad get a job alongside him at the *Forward* and Dad learned a new trade—he became a typesetter. While the pay was not high—Dad usually worked six days a week and never made more than $15,000 a year—it was steady work and there were benefits and a pension. Our parents did without eating out, vacations, a car or carpeting. Our mother often sewed her own clothes.

We moved to an apartment house in Crown Heights, Brooklyn on Empire Boulevard between Rogers and Nostrand Avenues and lived there from 1953-1956. Our parents tried to give us as normal an American childhood as possible. Dad took Al to Ebbets Field where they watched soccer and baseball games and our parents took both of us to Prospect Park where we went to the zoo and the merry-go-round and to the Brooklyn Botanical Gardens.

Our parents had been in the country for ten years before they could afford to buy the modest, semi-attached two family home in Midwood at 908 East 12th Street, Brooklyn, New York where they would spend the rest of their lives. This is where they finally put down roots in 1956 and we were raised. Dad was active in the neighborhood *shuls*—the Jewish Communal Center and the East Midwood Jewish Center—and was fondly called the "mayor" of East 12th Street. In his later years, Dad would say that he was rich, explaining that he had a roof over his head, his family and (once the mortgages on the house were paid) he didn't owe anyone money.

Our parents' Holocaust experiences permeated almost everything in their lives. Most of the people Dad worked with in his shop were fellow survivors. Dad and Mom spoke with accents, as did their close friends, most of whom were former Bielski Brigade members. When they got together, inevitably, they would talk about the War. Mom had nightmares about the Nazi slaughter and since Dad was a heavy sleeper, we were the ones who often woke her up. Thunder and lightning frightened Mom, reminding her of the German bombings.

Their lives revolved largely around us—their children. As children, we communicated with Dad in Yiddish. If we would respond to a question in English, he would say, *"Red Yiddish."* — "Speak Yiddish." Growing up, we never really understood what our parents had experienced. We would ask our parents why our friends at school from American homes had grandparents and lots of aunts and uncles and cousins but we did not. They always told us the truth. Nevertheless, when we were little, if our friends' parents had accents, we liked to think of them and their children as cousins.

Although life was a serious matter for our parents, they made sure that our lives were filled with happiness and celebrations as much as possible. Our bar mitzvahs were grand affairs, with large *kiddushim* at the house that our Mom spent weeks preparing and cooking for.

On the afternoon of Ralph's bar mitzvah, Tuvia Bielski came over. He and his wife Lilka and their children lived across the street from us. Ruth, Tuvia's daughter, had just made him a grandfather and he came in to celebrate both happy occasions with us. With the bar mitzvah food out on the table, Dad, Uncle Ben and Tuvia toasted and drank shots of whiskey. Not only were they celebrating a bar mitzvah and a birth—they were also celebrating their survival and continuation.

Mom worked hard to impart to us the old *shtetl* traditions. We had big Friday night dinners every week. Mom always *benched licht* (lit candles) and guests would often come to dinner. She was a wonderful cook and often cooked dishes that she remembered from life in the *shtetl*. She made wonderful *gefilte fish, knaidlach, kugels, lukshen, tzimis, gribiness and compot*. Among her special dishes were chicken croquettes (made from ground chicken breasts) and *zemel* (hamentash-like pastries). Among the cooking utensils she used in her preparations were two serving spoons and forks that she had had in her family home as a girl in Korelitz. Somehow, she had held on to them throughout her ordeal in the ghetto, the forest and the trek to America.

Making sure that we were well educated was our parents' top priority. They were never as proud as when Albert became a teacher, Ralph graduated from law school and Albert's children, Brian and Beth, graduated from college.

But the grandchildren were the real bonus. Nothing compared to the combination of love and joy on Mom and Dad's faces after Al and his wife Sharon brought their grandchildren Beth and Brian into the world. They were never happier or more at ease than when they were with their grandchildren.

As our parents grew older, they became ill and took care of one another with tenderness and tremendous patience. They were fighters to the end and were determined to live and die on their own terms. If the Nazis were to kill them, it would be with a "bullet to the back" by escaping rather than submitting. They valiantly fought back after diagnoses of heart attacks, cancer and other debilitating diseases. They died just as they lived—with courage and with dignity. Mom died first, on July 12, 1995; Dad died four years later, on March 23, 1999.

To our parents, being a *mentsch* was the highest virtue. In Yiddish a *mentsch* is a good person, one that does the right thing and helps others. Mom and Dad were proud when we acted like *mentschen*. But what is most amazing is that our parents were *mentschen* and that they were able to maintain their goodness, kindness and humanity in spite of all they went through.

Our parents felt strongly regarding educating others about those Jews who fought back during the Holocaust. They had come to see that their lives as partisan fighters were unique and that teaching others about their Holocaust experiences was not only important in terms of historic education, but their way of giving *koved*, i.e., honor, to their loved ones who were lost. It is our legacy to continue this mission and to tell their remarkable story.[xi]

The Story of Two Lives —
A Photo Album

Fruma as fortune teller in play for Korelitz Drama Circle, 1935.

Fruma's sisters Feigele, Grunia and daughter Mirele, and Brina before the war.

Murray (first on right) with cousins, Wseilub 1939-1940.

Sora Rivka, Murray Berger's mother, before the war.

Fruma with aunt Rivka Ullman and cousin Ephraim Gulkowich
(who died May, 1944 in the Tshalkos Brigade) - Korelitz, Poland, 1938.

Ben-Zion Gulkowich, 1930s.

Bielski Brigade fighters and members, 1943.
Fruma Gulkowich Berger- 3rd from right, first row.

Fruma, Yolanda Benson, Gootkeh
Nochomovski, Romania DP
camp, 1945.

Murray, Fruma and Elliot Berger,
Kibbutz Tulda, Romania,
1945.

Fruma (top row, first on left) and Murray Berger (to Fruma's left)
in Kibbutz Tulda DP camp in Romania, 1945.

Fruma (top row, fifth from right) and Murray Berger (top row, second from
right) at wedding in Kibbutz Tulda DP camp in Romania, 1945.

Partisans after the war - Kibbutz Tulda, Romania, 1945. Murray Berger, center first row, Fruma Berger, third row center.

Fruma & Ben-Zion in Rome, 1946.

Members of the Kibbutz Anzio, 1946-1947.

Ben-Zion and Judy Gulkow with son Albert, Rome, 1946.

Murray and Fruma, Rome, 1947.

Former Bielski partisans, Rome 1946-1947.

Wedding Picture, Rome, 1947.

Harry Berger, Murray's brother, who sponsored Murray and Fruma's immigration to America, Springfield, MA, early 1950s.

Murray and Fruma with
Hill and Orloff cousins,
Chicago, 1947.

Novogruder landsleit, New York, 1950s.

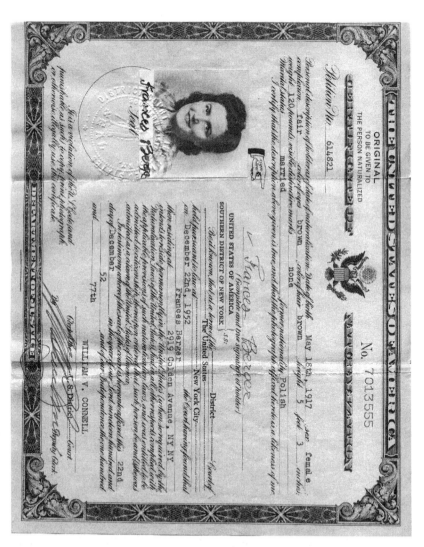

Fruma's American citizenship papers, 1952.

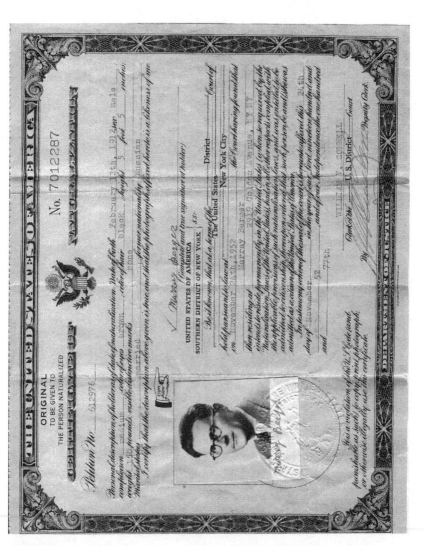

Murray's American citizenship papers, 1952.

Murray and Fruma at home, late 1940s-1950.

Murray, Albert and Fruma, 1950.

Fruma, Ralph, Albert and Murray at Ben's farm, 1955.

Murray working as a linotype operator, early 1960s.

Murray and Fruma dancing at Albert's bar mitzvah in 1960.

The Bergers and the Gulkows at Albert's bar mitzvah.

Murray and Fruma lighting candles at Albert's bar mitzvah.

Al's bar mitzvah—Standing from left-Lilka Bielski, Murray, Tuvia Bielski, Ruth Bielski, Fruma. Seated far right: Zus and Sonia Bielski.

Lilka and Tuvia Bielski lighting a candle at Albert's bar mitzvah.

Uncle Ellie and Aunt Rena at Ralph's bar mitzvah, August, 1965.

Sharon and Fruma, Brooklyn, 1973.

Murray and Fruma at
Al and Sharon's wedding,
August 8, 1971.

Fruma with Sharon and
granddaughter, Beth, 1976.

Fruma and Murray reunited with Fruma's Aunt Rivka and Uncle Louis
Ullman, Johannesburg, South Africa, 1972.

Fruma, Judy and Ben Gulkow, Al and Sharon Berger, Murray,
Brooklyn, 1977.

With South African cousins Sam and Leonie Pogorelsky - Brooklyn, 1977.

Murray with grandson, Brian, 1981.

Beth, Al, Fruma and Ralph – Brooklyn, 1981.

The Bergers' last family photo, taken at grandson Brian's
bar mitzvah – June 15, 1991.

Fork and spoon used by Fruma Gulkowitz, Bielski Family Camp, Naliboki forest, Poland, 1943-1944.

From the Museum of Jewish Heritage's exhibit, "Daring to Resist: Jewish Defiance in the Holocaust" (2007).

Ralph in Rome synagogue holding wedding ledger, 2006.

Memorial to Jews of Novogrudek and surrounding shtetls,
Novogrudek, Poland.

End Notes

[i] Nechama Tec, Defiance, (New York: Oxford University Press, 1993), pp.18, 25, 48.

[ii] Tec, 93

[iii] Tec 89-93

[iv] Robert Thurston & Bernd Benwetsch, eds., *The People's War* (Chicago: University of Illinois Press, 2000), pp. 40, 45

[v] Tec, 109

[vi] Ibid, 53,61

[vii] Wikipedia

[viii] Portions of this testimony have been previously published/recorded in a variety of formats including: "Women of Valor"/Center for Holocaust Studies - Volume 6, No. 4 Spring Issue 1990 Partisans and Resistance Fighters; "Partisans: A Personal Memoir", "Tears and Poems of a Jewish Woman" Shmulevitsch/Forwards Association, January 27, 1968; and Yale University/Fortunoff interview video.

[ix] Portions of the material in this section have been previously published or recorded in a variety of formats including "A Jew From The Forests" Shmulevitsch/Forwards Association, September 7, 1968; Anthology On Armed Jewish Resistance 1939-1945 (I. Kowalski ed. 1984); Yale University/ Fortunoff interview video; and Shoah Foundation interview video.

[x] Versions of these poems have been published in a variety of print venues including Martyrdom and Resistance, a bimonthly publication of the American Federation of Jewish Fighters, Camp Inmates and Nazi Victims, Inc. English translations of the poems were provided by Prof. Larry Gillig, Dr. Percy Matenko, Zelik Bedell, Sam Pogorelsky, Sheryl Kohl and Pearl Rochelson. The poems were edited by Prof. Larry Gillig and Ralph Berger. The versions presented in this section are based on those efforts.

[xi] Portions of this section were previously published in other sources, including "A Fighter to the End"/Geraldine Gross/The Jewish Week, July 28, 2000; and East Midwood Jewish Center Bulletin Vol. LXV, No 4, Dec 2004.

Sources

The following sources were consulted during the preparation of this book:

Kagan, Jack and Dov Cohen. Surviving the Holocaust with the Russian Jewish Partisans, 2nd Edition. London: Valentine Mitchell & Co. Ltd., 2000.

Levine, Allan, Fugitives of the Forest: The Heroic Story of Jewish Resistance and Survival During the Second World War. Stoddart, 1998.

Tec, Nechama. Defiance: The Bielski Partisans. New York: Oxford University Press, 1993.

Thurston, Robert & Bernd Benwetsch, eds. The People's War. Chicago: University of Illinois Press, 2000.

Glossary

Aktion – in German, an action or operation. When the Nazis attacked a ghetto, these *aktions* were accompanied by mass murder.

Aron Kodesh – The Holy Ark, where Torah scrolls are kept.

Chashmonaim – Maccabee fighters who defeated the Syrians and reclaimed the Temple at the time of the miracles of Chanukah.

Judenrat – German term for a Jewish council, appointed by the Germans and sometimes including prewar Jewish community leaders.

NKVD – Russian secret police.

Otriad – a partisan detachment that varied in size.

Partisans – members of a guerrilla band engaged in fighting or sabotage against an occupying army.

Shtetl – in Yiddish, small Jewish town or village formerly found in Eastern Europe.

Tallis, Tallit – a Jewish prayer shawl.

Teffilin – also called phylacteries, a pair of black leather boxes containing scrolls of parchment inscribed with verses from the Bible.

Kaddish – Jewish memorial service.

Yahrtzeit – Anniversary of the death of a loved one.

Yizkor – Jewish memorial prayer.

Ziemlankas – Polish term for dugouts, large camouflaged foxholes in which the partisans lived while in the forests.